The Human Predicament:

Towards an Understanding of the Human Condition

Max Malikow

The Human Predicament: Towards an Understanding of the Human Condition

Published by: Theocentric Publishing Group
1069A Main Street
Chipley, Florida 32428
http://www.theocentricpublishing.com

Library of Congress Control Number: 2013947807

ISBN 9780985618162

Dedications

To Rachel Joy Goodman, who wrote these words at age 13: "In this life we will come across many obstacles on the long road to true happiness. There is responsibility which limits us, lies which mislead us, desire which distracts us, and love which sustains us."

To George Raus: Good friends enrich life. Thank you for your generosity and friendship.

To Sharon Rene Martinez: Whose thoughtfulness extended well beyond her family. Her kindness is a precious memory.

To SC: Who made it through the rain and kept her point of view.

Acknowledgments

Acknowledgments are appropriate for books and a tonic for life in general. Giving others their due generates gratitude and gratitude is a prerequisite for overall life contentment. (Aristotle referred to such contentment as *eudaimonia.*) The ease with which twenty-three names came to mind when reflecting on contributors to this book was indeed gratifying.

There are those who have influenced my thinking over the years; their anonymous imprint (apart from this acknowledgement) is present in this book. They are Paul Bloom, Kay Jamison, Dan Keplinger, Fred "Mister" Rogers, Michael Schillace, and Douglas Stuart.

There are others who provided opportunities for research or occasions for reflection. Much of the content of the pages that follow is attributable to C. Tabor Fisher, Rabbi Earl Grollman, Sue Ellen Harris, John Hartung, Eric Holzwarth, Michael Kagan, and Mario Saenz.

Still others gave support and wisdom at times of personal distress. John Berthrong, the late Carmen DelCioppo, Jay Land, Michael Marcus, Joe Masterleo, Rico Petrocelli, and Father Robert Scully, S.J. each lent encouragement when my own human situation was a predicament.

A special note of appreciation is in order for Terry Riley and Karen White who furnished delightful venues in which early drafts of this book were produced.

Finally, I am indebted to Betsy Morgan, my editor and fact checker. Her excellent work was integral to the completion of this writing project.

Preface

To do philosophy is to explore one's own temperament, and yet at the same time to attempt to discover the truth.

-Iris Murdoch

I write to make sense of it all. That has not yet happened, so I keep on writing.

- JoAnne Windsinger

It cannot be known precisely when the writing of a book actually begins because locating the moment of an idea's conception is an impossibility. However, to an extent, why a book is written can be known. JoAnne Windsinger said she writes "to make sense of it all" (2012). Her explanation applies to this and every other book or article I've written. Concerning this treatise, I'm a human being engaged in an ongoing effort to make sense of myself, the events around me, and the people who intersect my life.

A less conceptual and more immediate explanation for this book is a course I teach at LeMoyne College in Syracuse, New York: "Philosophy 201: Philosophical Reflections on the Human Situation." Although taught by several professors, we all address a fundamental question: *Regardless of when and where people live (or have lived), are human beings more alike or dissimilar?*

The Dalai Lama, Buddhism's spiritual leader, cast his vote for "more alike" with these words:

> Some years ago the body of a Stone Age man was recovered from the ice of the European Alps. Despite being more than five thousand years old, it was perfectly preserved. Even its clothes were largely intact. I

remember thinking at that time were it possible to bring this individual back to life for a day, we would find that we have much in common with him. No doubt we would find that he too was concerned for his family and loved ones, for his health and so on. Differences of culture and expression notwithstanding, we would still be able to identify with one another on the level of feeling. And there could be no reason to suppose any less concern with finding happiness and avoiding suffering on his part than on ours. (1999, 220-221).

The eminent Harvard social psychologist Roger Brown expressed an opposing view in his memoir:

> As a psychologist, in all the years ... I had thought individual differences in personality were exaggerated. I compared personality psychologists to cultural anthropologists who took pleasure in, and indeed derived status from, the exoticism of their discoveries. I had once presumed to say to Henry A. Murray, Harvard's distinguished personologist: "I think people are all very much the same." Murray's response had been: "Oh you do, do you? Well, you don't know what the hell you're talking about!" And I hadn't. (1996, 169).

Given the mission of this book, it is appropriate to quote these two authorities, one from religion and the other from psychology. A consideration of the human condition requires input from these and other disciplines, including philosophy.

Perhaps the most important word in this book's title is "towards," implying a direction rather than a destination. No single work of any breadth or length could provide a comprehensive explanation of the uniqueness of human beings in the pantheon of living things. “Towards” expresses that these pages are intended as a contribution to an understanding of the implications of being human. Unlike JoAnne Windsinger, I am not trying “to make sense of it all.” Rather, I am trying to make sense of my life by considering it in the context of all lives.

Max Malikow
March 2, 2012
Syracuse, New York

Table of Contents

Introduction: What Is the Human Predicament?

My mother groaned, my father wept, into the dangerous world I leapt.

-William Blake

Strange is our situation upon earth. Each of us comes for a short visit, not knowing why, yet sometimes seeming to divine a purpose.

-Albert Einstein

It is not unusual for the title of a book to change as the writing project progresses. One of several working titles for this book was *The Human Situation* until it became apparent that "situation" is a neutral word and, therefore, inadequately descriptive. "Situation" was replaced by "predicament" owing to the latter's more precise depiction of a status that is not merely a circumstance, but one that is difficult, troubling, and, perhaps, perplexing. The social philosopher Eric Hoffer has described the human condition as more plight than pleasure:

> It is the individual only who is timeless. Societies, cultures, and civilizations – past and present – are often incomprehensible to outsiders, but the individual's hungers, anxieties, dreams, and preoccupations have remained unchanged through the millenia. Thus, we are up against the paradox that the individual who is more complex, unpredictable, and mysterious than any communal entity is the one nearest to our understanding; so near that even the interval of millenia

> cannot weaken our feeling of kinship. If in some manner the voice of an individual reaches us from the remotest distance of time, it is a timeless voice speaking about ourselves (1973, 81).

The twenty essays in this collection are divided into three subcategories. The first seven essays concern constitutional questions, addressing *how we are made*. The next eight concern operational questions, addressing *how we feel and behave.* The last five concern cognitive questions, speaking to *our mental processing.* Given the material presented in these essays, each one constituting a chapter, a response to the question, *What is the meaning of life?* provides a suitable epilogue.

Typical philosophical and psychological topics contemplated in this collection are the free will/determinism debate, moral relativism, abnormal behavior, happiness as the ultimate motivation, the reasonableness of belief in God, the experience of sensual pleasure, methods for establishing truth, human capacities for self-knowledge and change, sex, love, dreaming, learning, thinking, justice, humor, death, and life as meaningful or meaningless.

Psychiatrist and philosopher Irvin Yalom has posited there are four life issues that manifest in psychotherapy. His observation provides an efficient summary of the topics confronted in the pages ahead.

1. We carry the burden of responsibility that accompanies free will.
2. There is no apparent meaning to life.
3. There are parts of us that never will be disclosed to anyone else. Hence, we are never fully known to anyone.
4. We live with an ongoing awareness of our eventual death.

Martin Heidegger, an existentialist, characterized our entrance into the world as thrownness – cast into a life of frustrations, sufferings, and demands. Further, he believed it is our responsibility to respond to our individual situations by making choices and acting, making us answerable for the consequences that emanate from our behavior.

Another existentialist, although he denied he belonged in this category, is Albert Camus. His writing, especially two of his novels, *The Stranger* and *The Plague*, feature what he referred to as the first truth: the absurdity of our existence. He viewed "the confrontation and conflict between our rational expectations of the world (justice, satisfaction, and happiness) and the "indifference of the world" as absurd (Solomon, 2000, 91). His collection of essays, *The Myth of Sisyphus*, begins with this stunning thought: "There is but one truly serious philosophical problem, and that is suicide. Judging whether life is or is not worth living amounts to answering the fundamental question of philosophy" (1955, 3). In these essays, Camus employs Sisyphus, condemned by the Olympian gods to spend eternity in fruitless labor, as representative of all of us since we all spend a lifetime engaged in futile quests.

Ironic is that Camus, a deeply contemplative man, saw reflection as a problem because it leads us to question the ultimate value of our work and accomplishments. This sentiment is expressed in the song "Dust in the Wind," recorded by the group Kansas: "All we do crumbles to the ground though we refuse to see. Dust in the wind – all we are is dust in the wind" (Livgren, 1977).

Even if these dismal assessments by Heideggar and Camus are only partially valid, they are sufficient to justify the human situation as a predicament. Of course, they are not the only commentators on the human condition. Viktor Frankl, also an existentialist, Carl Jung, Aristotle, and Socrates are among those who believe a flourishing life is attainable through self-examination, personally meaningful work, and intimate relationships.

For each of us, if life is to be experienced as worthwhile, if not thrilling, and occasionally pleasant, if not joyful, our diligence is required. Even the most enviable of lives includes challenges, disappointments, frustrations, and confusions. There is a word for circumstances that challenge, disappoint, frustrate, and confuse us – that word is predicament. For this reason it is part of this book's title: *The Human Predicament: Towards an Understanding of the Human Condition.*

Constitutional Questions: How We Are Made

1. What Is a Human Being?

What a piece of work is man! How noble in reason! How infinite in faculty! In form and moving how express and admirable! In action, how like an angel! In apprehension, how like a god! The beauty of the world, the paragon of animals; and yet to me, what is this quintessence of dust? Man delights not me; no, nor woman neither; though by your smiling you seem to say so.

- Hamlet, Act II, scene 2

For you created me in my inmost being; you knit me together in my mother's womb, I praise you because I am fearfully and wonderfully made; your works are wonderful, I know that full well.

-Psalm 139: 13,14

The two quotations above express estimations of human beings that are in diametric opposition. Speaking through Hamlet, Shakespeare is not in the least impressed with us. To the contrary, the psalmist, King David, characterizes us as divine creatures to be regarded with admiration and awe. Which are we? What are we to conclude about our species that includes both Jeffrey Dahmer, a serial murderer and cannibal, and Mother Teresa, an altruistic Nobel laureate? It seems the same capacities that empower us to behave nobly also enable us to act dishonorably.

One means for addressing the question, "What is a human being?" is to compare and contrast us to things that are *human-like* but not actually human. On May 6. 1997 reigning world chess champion Garry Kasparov competed against an IBM computer named "Deep Blue" in a six game match. Kasparov won one game, lost one game, and played to a tie in three others. Kasparov lost the sixth, tie-breaking game. How was the experience of playing chess different for Kasparov than his computer opponent?

In *Witchdoctors and Psychiatrists* (1986) E. Fuller Torrey wondered if a computer could function as a psychiatrist. He hypothesized such therapy would take some form of the following interaction:

> Computer: Hello, please tell me your name.
> Me: Torrey.
> Computer: It's nice to meet you, Torrey. I would like to discuss your problem with you. Please tell me first whether you are male or female.
> Me: Male.
> Computer: How old are you?
> Me: Thirty-two.
> Computer: Are you married?
> Me: Yes.
> Computer: Now, how can I help you?
> Me: I don't know.
> Computer: Tell me something about your wife.
> Me: She is a fine wife. We have a good marriage.
> Computer: I understand. Now tell me something about your parents.
> Me: My father is dead. My mother has been sick.
> Computer: Tell me more about her.
> Me: She is getting better now.
> Computer: Does your wife tend to be like your mother?
> Me: No, not at all.
> Computer: I understand. Now let me ask you something else about your mother. Was she very strict in raising you?
> Me: No, she was lenient. I made all my own decisions.

> Computer: Does it bother you that you made all your own decisions?
> Me: No, I like to.
> Computer: Why do you like to?
> Me: Because then I have created my own existential meaning.
> Computer: I understand. Please tell me more about someone close to you.
>
> (I wasn't certain if the computer *did* understand or not. I decided to test it and see how it handled hostility.)
>
> Me: Why are you so insensitive?
> Computer: I am doing my best under these conditions.
> Me: You are just a crazy machine.
> Computer: You seem interested in me personally.
> Me: Who do you think you are?
> Computer: Please think of me as a doctor trying to discuss your feelings about people close to you. Call me anything you wish (36-37).

Both IBM "Deep Blue" and Torrey's "computer psychiatrist" lacked self-awareness. Gary Kasparov and E. Fuller Torrey knew they were men engaged with a computer. Neither computer was aware of itself as a computer interacting with a human being.

Personality is "an individual's characteristic pattern of thinking, feeling, and acting" (Myers, 2010, 553). Torrey believes the personality of the therapist is one of the basic components of effective psychotherapy (35). Lacking the capacity to experience emotion, a computer cannot be said to have a personality. Describing his therapeutic experience with a computer, Torrey reflected:

> We went through an extensive history of my childhood, illnesses, the kind of women who attract me, the kind of men I admire, etc. The computer seemed interested in me and apparently wanted to help, was strangely like a therapist, and evoked feelings of both fascination and disquiet (37).

A lack of feeling is integral to the plot of the science fiction movie, "I, Robot." Set in the year 2035, Will Smith is in the role of a detective who strongly dislikes the robots that have been developed to serve human beings by doing their menial labor. The reason for this aversion is an automobile accident in which Smith's character (Del Spooner) was driving across a bridge when he was hit by another car. Both cars fell into the water below and were sinking fast. A robot jumped into the water and rescued Spooner, who was protesting, trying to redirect the robot to save an eleven year-old girl in the other car. Devoid of emotion, the robot responded: "Your probability of survival is 45 percent; the child's probability is 11 percent" (Twentieth Century Fox, 2004). The girl drowned.

The eighteenth century German philosopher Immanuel Kant reduced the study of philosophy to four questions, one of which is: *What is a human being?* A later philosopher, William James, had this question in mind when he created the problem of the "mechanical sweetheart." A thought experiment, it describes the perfect lover, ideal in every respect, including stunning physical beauty. James posed this question: *What if after falling in love you learned the "sweetheart" was actually an android and not a human being?* This leads to other questions: *Would this awareness make a difference, since it could not have been discovered by anything detectable by your senses? Further, what would the android be missing? A spirit? A soul? What are they? And, if they exist, how do they make human beings different from androids?*

One response to the question of the difference between a human being and an android is the difference between each saying, "I love you." The android's expression would come from programming; the human being's declaration would be driven by an emotion. In addition, the programmed android would have no choice but to say, "I love you." A human being could choose not to say it. While there is no disputing that human beings experience emotions, there is a long history of dispute among philosophers and psychologists as to whether or not human beings actually possess free will. Concerning this matter, Samuel Johnson observed: "All theory is against the freedom of the will; all experience for it" (Boswell, 2008, 273). The issue of free will is addressed at length in chapter three.

Human beings are distinguished from all other organisms in that they have self-awareness, experience emotions, and, possibly, exercise free will. In the poem "An Essay on Man," Alexander Pope directs each of us to enrich our self-awareness by examining our emotions and thoughts. He believed this to be a more fruitful deployment of intellectual energy:

> Know then thyself, presume not God to scan; The proper study of mankind is man" (1733).

Similarly, Socrates taught, "An unexamined life is not worth living" (Plato, 399 B.C., 38a). The maxim "know thyself" was inscribed in the forecourt of the Temple of Apollo at Delphi. Computers and androids are incapable of introspection and self-understanding. They cannot be curious about feelings they do not have or actions that did not originate with them. Another means for pursuing an answer to Kant's question is to compare human beings to animals by considering whether human beings have an ethical obligation to treat animals humanely. The renown humanitarian Albert Schweitzer wrote: "To the person who is truly ethical all life is sacred, including that which from the human point of view seems lower. ... Will the time ever come when public opinion will no longer tolerate popular amusements that depend on the maltreatment of animals!" (1933, 235-237). In his essay, "Consider the Lobster," David Foster Wallace questioned the culinary practice of submerging lobsters in boiling water:

> So then here is a question that is all but unavoidable ... and may arise in kitchens across the U.S: Is it right to boil a sentient creature alive just for our gustatory pleasure? A related set of concerns: Is the previous question irksomely PC or sentimental? What does "all right" even mean in this context? Is the whole thing just a matter of personal choice? As you may or may not know, a certain well-known group called People for the Ethical Treatment of Animals thinks that the morality of lobster-boiling is not just a matter of individual conscience (243).

To be fair, Wallace presents the argument that the nervous system of the lobster does not include a cerebral cortex, "which in humans is the area of the brain that gives the experience of pain" (245). Still, he concludes, "Since pain is a totally subjective mental experience, we do not have direct access to anyone or anything's pain but our own" (246).

If human beings have an ethical obligation to animals this has implications for what it means to be human. The word *humane* is defined as, "having the good qualities of human beings, as kindness, mercy, or compassion" (*American Heritage Dictionary*, 1973, 640). When Robert Burns wrote, "Man's inhumanity to man makes countless thousands mourn" he was expressing dismay at our capacity for orchestrating pain and suffering on each other (1784). It is tautological that we have no expectation of *humane* behavior from animals. In contrast to animals, the free will debate notwithstanding, we are expected to comport ourselves with civility and in accordance with a moral code. Further, we are responsible for the foreseeable consequences of our actions. To this point, the philosopher Thomas Ellis Katen has posited:

> Human beings come to terms with life and understand themselves as human through such experiences as regret, remorse, sorrow, and guilt. This entire mode of functioning cannot be simply discounted. Free will is a working assumption of human existence as it has evolved throughout history, and moral experience is an all-important aspect of that history. Precisely because human experience over the course of history does found itself on a premise of freedom, we have an excellent working criterion on the basis of which we might justify free will. ... Since determinism itself is only a theory and not an established fact about the universe, why should we deny our experience of freedom? (1973, 318).

Conclusion

This chapter expresses an attempt to answer the question, "What is a human being?" The comparison between computers and human beings demonstrates that the former lacks the characteristics of self-awareness, emotions, and free will (if it exists). William James' "mechanical sweetheart" thought experiment raises the following questions concerning the composition of human beings: Do we have a spirit or soul? If we do, how would this be a distinguishing human characteristic? Finally, even if human beings have an ethical obligation to treat animals with consideration, animals have no ethical obligation to reciprocate. By definition, *humane* treatment is required of human beings because only human beings can provide it.

Genesis, the first book of the Hebrew Bible, includes this narrative: "So God created man in his own image, in the image of God he created him; male and female he created them" (Genesis 1:27). What does it mean for man and woman to have been created in the image of God? Theologian David Wells interprets the *imago dei* to mean human beings are "cognitive, reflective egos" (1982). Wells believes we have God's qualities without God's quantities. As cognitive beings, we can acquire knowledge, but we will never be omniscient. We are capable of reflection, but our thoughts will never be as profound as God's:

> "For my thoughts are not your thoughts, neither are your ways my ways," declares the Lord. "As the heavens are higher than the earth, so are my ways higher than your ways and my thoughts than your thoughts" (Isaiah 55:8,9).

And we can develop self-knowledge (ego), without ever fully understanding ourselves.

2. Is Each of Us Unique?

"All of us are related, each of us is unique."

- Anonymous

O Lord ... you are familiar with all my ways. ... All the days ordained for me were written in your book before one of them came to be.

-Psalm 139: 1,3, 16

What is man that you make so much of him, that you give him so much attention?

- Job 7:17

In his *Discourse on Metaphysics* the German philosopher Gottfried Leibniz (1686) delivers good news to narcissists – those who need continual assurance that they are special. Leibniz's *identical principle* (also known as "Leibniz's Law") effectively reasons that no two things are identical. He posited that two things are identical only if everything that is true about a is also true of b. Hence, even monozygotic twins are not identical since their times of birth are different, even if the day of their birth is the same. Further, they do not have the same names. (With this argument, Leibniz also proved that no two snowflakes are alike since no two of them fall to earth at exactly the same spot at precisely the same time.)

Each of us is unique! Each of us inhabits a body shared with no one else. The allotment is one body per person; no more and no less. (Conjoined twins being a rare exception to this allocation.) As stated in the previous chapter, personality is defined as, "an individual's characteristic pattern of thinking, feeling, and acting" (Myers, 2010, 553).

Since the contributors to personality are nature and nurture and each of us has a DNA and personal history that is singular, we are unique in personality.

Still another way in which each of us is particular is with regard to being and time. Martin Heidegger's *Being and Time* provides what many believe to be the most difficult reading in philosophical literature (1927). The basic idea of his treatise is human beings exist temporally between birth and death. Being is time and time for each of us is finite – ending for each of us with our death. Therefore, to have *authenticity*, which is Heidegger's term for "genuine human existence," we must live with a constant awareness of our death. This notion of living with cognizance of death is Heidegger's *being-towards-death*. He believed our time and location in human history and whatever resources and opportunities we have constitute our unique sphere of influence. Heidegger believed that since we are defined by our accomplishments and they are limited by time and place it follows that *being and time* provide the venue in which we authenticate ourselves.

The story of Billy Miske, an American prize fighter, amply exemplifies authenticity and being-towards-death. In 1918 his doctor diagnosed him with Bright's disease and estimated that Billy was going to die from kidney failure in approximately five years. Deeply in debt, Miske continued boxing until the disease made fighting an impossibility.

By the fall of 1923, Billy is dying fast. ... He's too weak to work out, much less prizefight. The only thing thinner than Billy's arms is his wallet. He hasn't had a bout since January, which is trouble, because Christmas is coming up fast (Reilly, 12/27/1999).

Nevertheless, he was determined that the last Christmas with his wife and three children is going to be special. Barely able to get out of bed, he was able to convince his manager to arrange a fight, which undoubtedly would be

Billy's last. Unable to train, he shows up for the fight and earns $2,400 for four rounds of work. (He won the fight by a knockout!)

The check buys the best Christmas the Miskes ever have. The kids come flying downstairs in the morning ... to presents stacked higher than they can reach. They eat like Rockefellers and sing like angels and laugh all day (Reilly).

One week later, on New Years Day 1924, Billy Miske died of kidney failure in a Minneapolis hospital. Of course, some may question Billy's judgment, citing his life-shortening decision to continue fighting. His place in this treatise is as a real-life instantiation of Heideggerian existentialism in which a human being's existence is authenticated by action taken with a full awareness of death. In addition, Billy Miske was a unique human being. He lived at a certain place with singular responsibilities and resources (*being*) at a specific location in human history (*time*) thereby giving him a limited sphere of influence.

As stated previously, Albert Camus wrote: "There is but one truly serious philosophical problem and that is suicide. Judging whether life is or is not worth living amounts to answering the fundamental question of philosophy" (1955, 3). The point he made with this stark analysis is that the primary question for each of us is to decide if the life we are living is worthy of the effort to live it. If the answer is "no," then suicide is the logical course of action. If the answer is "yes," then each of us has to determine the personal actions that will make life meaningful.

Psychiatrist Gordon Livingston has made a surprising disclosure about his work with suicidal patients:

> When confronted with a suicidal person I seldom try to talk them out of it. Instead I ask them to examine what it is that has so far dissuaded them from killing themselves. Usually this involves finding out what the

> connections are that tether that person to life in the face of nearly unbearable psychic pain (2004, 71-72).

Livingston is suggesting yet another way in which we are unique: our unmatched constellation of relationships – the connections that tether us to this life. With these relationships come experiences and responsibilities available to no other person. Walt Whitman expressed this sentiment poetically in "O Me! O Life!:"

> O me! O life! ... of the questions of these recurring; Of the endless trains of the faithless – of cities filled with the foolish; Of myself forever reproaching my-self (for who more foolish than I, and who more faith-less?) ... Of the empty and useless years of the rest – with the rest me intertwined; The question, O me! So sad, recurring -- What good amid these, O me, O life?

Answer:

> That you are here – that life exists, and identity; That the powerful play goes on and you will contribute a verse (2000, 298).

Shakespeare wrote, "All the world's a stage" (1623). Like Whitman, he used the metaphor of a play to characterize life. Whitman saw us as authors who contribute a verse; Shakespeare saw us as players with exits and entrances playing many parts. Both imply that each of us is unique in our contribution to the great play.

Conclusion

Unique is an adjective, defined as, "being the only one of its kind...without an equal or equivalent" (*American*

Heritage Dictionary, 1969, 1400). In the number of ways presented in this essay, all of us qualify as unique. However, it would be gratuitous to claim that uniqueness proves that we are important and/or our lives have significance. (The issue of the meaning of life is addressed separately in the epilogue.)

The German word *Weltanschauung* is translated into English as "world view" and refers to an individual's comprehensive conception of the world. What each of us concludes about our uniqueness will be determined by our *Weltanschauung*. As expressed in his famous soliloquy, Macbeth's overall view of life is that it is tedious, senseless, brief, and, ultimately, meaningless.

> To-morrow and to-morrow and to-morrow,
> Creeps in this petty pace from day to day,
> To the last syllable of recorded time;
> And all our yesterdays have lighted fools
> The way to dusty death. Out, out, brief candle!
> Life's but a walking shadow, a poor player
> That struts and frets his hour upon the stage
> And then is heard no more. It is a tale
> Told by an idiot, full of sound and fury
> Signifying nothing (Shakespeare, 1611).

The implication of Macbeth's discourse is that even if we are unique our existence is nevertheless fatuous, inconsequential, and temporary.

In contrast, the biblical view expressed in the *New Testament* is, "we are God's workmanship, created in Christ Jesus to do good works, which God prepared in advance for us to do" (Ephesians 2:10). The Greek word behind the English "workmanship" is *poiema*, from which the word "poem" derives. Commentators have posited that this verse characterizes each of us as a divine masterpiece, uniquely equipped for the specific work God has in mind for each us.

In between these extreme world views is the existentialist position. While there are many subcategories of this philosophy, the thread running through all of them is that life *can* have meaning, but it is each person's responsibility to determine for herself what will constitute a meaningful life.

3. Do We Have Free Will?

Men believe themselves to be free simply because they are conscious of their own actions, knowing nothing of the causes by which they are determined.

- Benedict Spinoza

Triggers are pulled by individuals. Orders are given and executed by individuals. In the last analysis, every single human act is ultimately the result of an individual.

- Scott Peck

Without freedom there can be no morality.

- Carl Jung

We have to believe in free will. We've got no choice.

- Isaac Bashevis Singer

Over two hundred years ago the French philosopher Paul Holbach wrote:

> Man's life is a line that nature commands him to describe upon the surface of the earth, without his ever being able to swerve from it, even for an instant. ... Nevertheless, in spite of the shackles by which he is bound, it is pretended that he is a free agent. (1770, 1).

This is an uncompromising statement of *determinism*, "the position ... that every event is the necessary outcome of a cause or set of causes" (Katen, 1973, 313). So defined, it would seem that determinism makes no provision for *free will*, "the capacity of human beings to make choices free of coercion or compulsion and to choose the important actions of their lives" (Pence, 2000, 23).

The belief that people have the ability to make authentic selections from options is not derived from experimentation, hence it is not an empirically based position. Also, since belief in free will is not the result of a sound reasoning process, it is not based upon logic. The appeal of free will emanates from emotion and experience. William James, in his essay, "The Dilemma of Determinism," argued for free will on the premise that the experiences of guilt and regret make sense only if people believe they could have acted otherwise. An appealing, if not compelling, case for free will is made by Tom Morris with these words:

> We make decisions every day. What do I want for breakfast? What should I wear today? Which tie goes best with this suit? Should I go shopping before dinner or after? Is today the day to have that difficult conversation with a coworker that I've been putting off?
>
> The fact that we deliberate and think of ourselves as deciding what to do in many ways throughout the day demonstrates that we think of ourselves as having real options. We think of ourselves as having choices. We conceive of ourselves as being free.
>
> A belief in free will is being supposed by all of traditional morality. We praise people for their good deeds and blame them for the bad that they do. But praise and blame make no sense unless people have real choices (1999, 125).

Determinists counter the sentimentalist argument represented by James and Morris by pointing out that it is not unusual for people to feel guilty about events over which they admit to having had no control. Further, since every effect has a cause, it might be that human beings are compelled to have these emotions for reasons that are unknown and might not ever be discovered. (Determinists posit that there are three categories of causes: the causes that are known; those that eventually will be known; and those that never will be known.)

The problem of "(whether) human beings can be said to be free agents or whether their activities and thoughts are determined completely by the many influencing factors that impinge on them" constitutes the *free will problem* (Popkin and Stroll, 1981, 115). Stated as a question, the free will problem asks: *Why are people held responsible for behaviors over which they had no control?* Introduced as a dilemma, the free will problem presents this paradox: *Across cultures and time, human beings are held responsible for their behavior. Also, given the law of cause-and-effect, it is logical that the sequence of causes that culminates in a given behavior is beyond the control of the individuals, making them not responsible for their behavior.*

Essential to a consideration of the free will problem is an understanding of two subcategories of determinism: hard determinism and soft determinism:

> Hard determinism maintains that all behavior is invariably and without exception determined by causal forces beyond the control and responsibility of any individual, so that, in effect, free will and moral choice do not exist. However, soft determinism ... maintains that while there is a cause for all action, certain choices can still be made freely as actions that stem from the character or will of the agent, thus preserving the notion of moral responsibility (Pence, 14).

Is the free will problem an *antinomy*, "the existence of two incompatible statements, each of which taken alone is reasonable" (Pence, 3), or a *conundrum*, "a problem admitting of no satisfactory solution" (Morris, 1969, 290)? Aristotle's axiom that the truth of a matter is to be found between two extreme positions suggests the concept of soft determinism might contribute to a solution. Soft determinism, also referred to as *compatibilism*, allows for both determinism and free will to be in play. Of course, such a meeting of east and west requires an elaboration, which is the charge of the balance of this chapter.

The Significance of the Free Will Problem

Approximately one-thousand years ago the Persian poet Jalalu'ddin Rumi observed: "There is a disputation that will continue till mankind are raised from the dead, between the necessitarians and the partisans of free will" (Feinberg and Shafer-Landeau, 2002, 499). That observation is no less true today than it was in the twelfth century. The longevity of the *free will – determinism* disputation is attributable to its implications for civil order, criminal culpability, interpersonal relationships, and the experience of guilt. In his essay, "The Problem of Free Will," Walter Stace accurately characterized the free will problem as a debate that is semantic rather than pragmatic:

> It is to be observed that those learned professors of philosophy or psychology who deny free will do so only in their own professional moments and in their studies and lecture rooms. For when it comes to doing anything practical, even of the most trivial kind, they invariably behave as if they and others were free (Fineberg and Shafer-Landeau, 487).

Richard Popkin and Avril Stroll made a similar argument against determinism with this simple, but not simplistic, observation:

> If the determinist's theory is true, then instead of propounding arguments, he/she ought to find out what factors produce philosophical decisions, and then employ these, whether they be wooden clubs, alcoholic beverages, drugs, etc. But the fact that he/she, too, uses argumentation suspects there is some element of freedom in human behavior. Also, if one takes determinism seriously, anyone who believes in free will is determined to accept that theory, so what possible good could reasonable discussion accomplish? (1993, 120).

"What is a human being?" is one of four questions Immanuel Kant put forward as seminal and indispensable to philosophy (1998, 28). Thomas Katen provides a partial answer to Kant's question with his assertion that free will is a distinguishing feature of human beings:

> Which makes most sense of and best illuminates the facts of human experience as we know them? If the issue is put in these terms, I think the position could be developed that the idea of freedom is an inherent part of the defining concept of man (1973, 318).

This is not to claim that an individual acting under coercion or handicapped by a mental illness is not a human being. To the contrary, in criminal proceedings such conditions are considered extenuating circumstances, contextualizing an act in the interest of giving the accused full consideration as a human being. Conversely, people who are being manipulated or lied to are not receiving full consideration as human beings. Victims of manipulation or lies are unaware of some of the influences on their behavior and are thus deprived of an optimal exercise of free will.

Harry Frankfurt of Princeton University has provided another partial answer to the question: "What is a human being?" He taught that free will is to be understood in a hierarchical manner. The first-order of free will is the ability to act on a desire. The second-order of free will is unique to human beings: "An act is free if it is in accord with the desire one wants to desire" (Grim, 2008, 148). Frankfurt would make a distinction between alcoholics have a desire to drink but do *not* want that desire, and alcoholics who desire to drink and are untroubled by that desire. The former *are not* free because they have a craving they wish they did not have. Since they do not want to be alcoholics their yearning for alcohol is contrary to their will. The latter *are* free because their desire to drink is acceptable to them. Having accepted their alcoholism, they are not drinking against their will.

To better understand the difference between deliberate acts of free will and non-thinking action, consider instances of creatures acting instinctively. The eminent entomologist E.O. Wilson accomplished a fascinating experiment following his discovery that living ants react to dead ants according to a chemical message. Wilson learned that two days after an ant dies, the deceased insect emits the odor of oleic acid. A living ant passing by a dead comrade interprets the odor as a signal to remove the corpse to the colony's burial area. Wilson was able to produce a substance with the odor of oleic acid, which he then sprayed on a live ant. As he expected, the next ant passing by the ant he had sprayed set about to remove the "dead" ant to the burial site. The sprayed ant resisted the premature funeral, vigorously fighting off the ant attempting to make the removal to the final resting place. (One can only wonder how the sprayed ant interpreted the odor of oleic acid.)

Similarly, Robert Cialdini reported the research of M.W. Fox, who noted an innate behavior among turkeys – specifically turkey mothers.

> Turkey mothers are good mothers – loving, watchful, and protective. ...But there is something odd about their method. Virtually all of this mothering is triggered by one thing: the "cheep-cheep" sound of young baby chicks. ... If a chick makes the "cheep-cheep" noise, its mother will care for it; if not, the mother will ignore or sometimes kill it (1984, 2).

Polecats are natural enemies of turkeys and the approach of a polecat will drive a turkey into a frenzy of squawking, clawing, and pecking. In Fox's experiment he placed a stuffed polecat in the proximity of a mother turkey and drew it toward her by pulling on an attached string. As expected, the mother turkey reacted with a furious attack.

> When however the same stuffed polecat carried inside it a small recorder that played the "cheep-cheep" sound of baby turkeys, the mother not only accepted the oncoming polecat but gathered it underneath her. When the machine was turned off, the polecat model again drew a vicious attack (2).

In recent years considerable attention has been given to pheromones, chemical signals that trigger a reaction to another member of the same species. A possibility that has not been confirmed by research is that pheromones play a significant role in the attraction of one human being to another. If pheromones are a factor in romantic attraction then the role of conscious choice-making is diminished. While this would not relegate people to the same deterministic status as ants and turkeys, it does have implications for the understanding of free will. Some researchers are suggesting that the selection of a partner might not be an uncontaminated free will choice (Fallon and Aron, 2001).

The free will problem is not a mere playground for philosophers. As previously stated, it is an integral part of any serious discussion of civil order, criminal responsibility, justice, interpersonal relationships, and the personal experience of guilt. In some situations, assigning responsibility to a person is not easily accomplished. The case of James Carncross is such an instance. On December 6, 2006 in Syracuse, New York a jury found the twenty-one year-old Carncross guilty of criminally negligent homicide in the death of New York State Trooper Craig Todeschini. Eight months earlier Todeschini was killed when he lost control of his SUV while in pursuit of Carncross, who was on a motorcycle evading the trooper at speeds in excess of one-hundred miles per hour. Criminal negligence is defined as having acted in such a way as to create a substantial and unjustifiable risk that an ordinary person would perceive as substantial and unjustifiable. (The jury did not find Carncross guilty of manslaughter: the killing of another with neither premeditation nor intention to kill.)

The trial of James Carncross raised a philosophical question that has reverberated through as many centuries as human beings have been thinking about their behavior: How is personal responsibility determined? It is one thing to say that people are responsible for their actions. Stated more precisely, people are responsible for the consequences of their actions. It is quite another thing to say that people are responsible for every event in a sequence that was initiated by something they have done. People are accountable for any and all foreseeable events that follow their actions and are connected to them. However, there is no formula for distinguishing foreseeable events from those that are unforeseeable. Making such a distinction is a matter of judgment.

The *law of unintended consequences* maintains that every significant action is followed by unplanned events (Merton, 1936). It is implicit in this law that statements like, "I didn't intend for X to happen," and "I never anticipated that X would happen," are inadequate for the relief of responsibility. People are responsible for the intentions and imaginable effects of their behavior. This being said, "I didn't mean for or anticipate that X would happen," is not the same thing as saying, "No one could not have imagined that X would happen."

Applying the law of unintended consequences to this case, is it reasonable to assume that Trooper Todeschini's death is one of the possibilities Carncross should have anticipated when he decided to take flight? Given the situation, it seems doubtful that he deliberated before attempting his escape. If he considered any possibilities, likely they included getting caught, getting away, or getting himself killed. To have anticipated the trooper's death, Carncross would have had to calculate that the trooper had no alternative means of pursuit and would not break-off the chase – even if it meant pursuing in excess of the SUV's maneuvering capability. Ironically – some might say criminally – Carncross took for granted the trooper's high-speed driving ability and good judgment in making pursuit. In other words, Carncross took for granted Todeschini's ability to take care of himself.

The jury agreed with the prosecution and Carncross was sentenced to seven years imprisonment to be followed by five years on probation. That he was responsible for initiating the high-speed chase is indisputable. That he should have anticipated the trooper's death is unclear. An indelicate question is: Does Todeschini bear some responsibility for his own death? At his sentencing, Carncross said, "Had I known then what I know now, I would have stopped" (The Post

Standard, 2/15/07). There is no hint of determinism in that statement. He believes that given different circumstances (i.e. more knowledge) he would have chosen to act differently Regarding crime and punishment, forensic psychiatrist Dorothy Otnow Lewis has likened free will to sanity in that both exist as a continuum:

> ... all or none standards of sanity and insanity don't do justice to the complexity of human behavior. ...Guilt was a lot easier to measure before we recognized that free will, like sanity and insanity, is a constantly fluctuating intellectual and emotional continuum and not a fixed, immutable capacity or state of mind (1998, 283-284).

In 1984 a young lawyer witnessed the testimony of a ten-year-old rape victim in the De Soto County courthouse in Hernando, Mississippi. The lawyer, John Grisham, based his first novel, A Time to Kill, on what would have happened if the girl's father had murdered her rapists. Legal defenses based on diminished capacity, temporary insanity, and crimes of passion give weight to Lewis' view that a human being's state of mind is subject to considerable variability. It is no simple matter to assign responsibility for a crime committed under stress so extraordinary that the defendant's state of mind was altered.

In a 1924 case hailed as "the trial of the century" Clarence Darrow served as the defense counsel for two young men who had abducted and murdered a fourteen-year-old boy. Darrow had the accused, Nathan Leopold and Richard Loeb, plead guilty and then argued for life imprisonment in lieu of their execution. Darrow argued that their state of mind had been altered by indoctrination into the philosophy of Friedrich Nietzsche. Nietzsche believed that men should create their own values rather than passively conform to societal standards. Darrow was successful in making the case that Leopold and Loeb were not fully responsible for their crime:

> Is any blame attached because somebody took Nietzsche's philosophy seriously and fashioned a life upon it? ... it is hardly fair to hang a 19 year-old boy for the philosophy that was taught him at a university (Darrow, 8/22/24).

Equally challenging is determining the culpability of individuals who have done something so horrifying that the act itself is a declaration of a mental illness. The psychiatric diagnosis of Edward Van Dyke will never be known, but there is no doubting that his state of mind was pathological. In the spring of 2006, while on vacation with his family in Florida, he threw his eight and four-year-old sons from the fifteenth floor balcony of their hotel room. Van Dyke, a physician, then jumped to his own death, making an explanation for this bizarre murder-suicide unavailable.

Even among those who have committed similar acts, there is diversity among their sentences. Sherwin Nuland's *How We Die* includes the horrifying, heart-breaking narrative of the murder of nine-year-old Katie Mason by Peter Carlquist, a paranoid schizophrenic man who was determined not responsible for his crime. Not so for Andrea Yates, who drowned her five children, ranging in age from six months to seven years. She was found guilty of capital murder in spite of her psychiatric history that included chronic and psychotic episodes accompanied by auditory hallucinations. (Convicted in 2002, her sentence was overturned in 2006, when she was found not guilty by reason of insanity and confined to a psychiatric institute.)

In *The Man Who Mistook His Wife for His Hat*, neurologist Oliver Sacks presents the case study of Donald, a man who was not held responsible for a murder. Although there was no question that he had committed the murder, Donald was neither executed nor sent to prison. Instead, he was incarcerated in a psychiatric hospital for the criminally insane.

> Donald killed his girl while under the influence of PCP. He had, or seemed to have, no memory of the deed – and neither hypnosis nor sodium amytal served to release any. There was, therefore, it was concluded when he stood trial, not a repression of memory, but an organic amnesia – the sort of blackout well described with PCP.
>
> The details, manifest on forensic examination, were macabre and could not be revealed in open court. They were discussed *in camera* – concealed from both the public and Donald himself. Comparison was made with acts of violence occasionally committed during temporal lobe or psychomotor seizures. There is no memory of such acts, and perhaps no intention of violence – those who commit them are considered neither responsible nor culpable, but are nonetheless committed for their own and others' safety. This was what happened with the unfortunate Donald (1970, 154).

In contrast to Donald is Arthur Shawcross, the "Genessee River Killer" convicted in 1990 of ten murders and sentenced to 250 years in prison. (Shawcross died in prison in 2008 at age 63.) Dorothy Otnow Lewis interviewed Shawcross and testified for the defense at his trial. In *Guilty by Reason of Insanity* she expresses her belief that there is a neurological explanation for his psychopathic behavior:

> ... the MRI had shown that, nestled at the tip of his right temporal lobe, was a small, fluid-filled cyst. The brain is a very sensitive organ. The tiniest scar or tumor or cyst can, under certain circumstances, trigger abnormal electrical activity. ... Abnormal electrical foci at the anterior pole of the temporal lobe have been associated with bizarre, animalistic behaviors. ...
>
> Mr. Shawcross never denied any of the murders to me. He admitted everything. The trouble was, whenever I tried to get a complete account of what he had done, Mr. Shawcross became befuddled. He would repeatedly confuse one murder with another. Finally, in desperation, I asked, "Mr. Shawcross, do you remember what happened?" "No. Not really." "Then why did you confess to the police?" He looked at me as though I were crazy. "because I was there!" (Lewis, 1998, 272)

Dr. Lewis' testimony did not establish an extenuating circumstance for the jury. Moreover, she was reviled by the media and public. Instead of being respected as a scientist and expert, she was maligned as being effusively sympathetic to a serial murderer:

> Not only did the jury not believe me, they hated me. Then again, so did the rest of Rochester (New York). ... Night after night during the course of my testimony I would return to my hotel room ... I would then switch on the news and watch the man (or woman) in the street belittle me and my testimony. ... It was a nightmare (280).

The Solution: Compatibilism

Is there a way out of this fly bottle or is any claim to a solution a futile attempt to have one's cake and eat it too? *Compatibilism* "claims that determinism and free will can both be true. In other words, every event may have a cause and I am still free to make my own choices" (Pence, 10). In "Freedom and Necessity" A.J. Ayer advocated for compatibilism as the solution to the free will problem:

> It seems that if we are to retain this idea of moral responsibility, we must either show that men can be held responsible for actions which they do not do freely, or else find some way of reconciling determinism with the freedom of the will (1969, 273).

Ayer and other compatibilists have located the problem in the confusion of two terms: *causation and coercion.* Compatibilism maintains that *causality equals coercion* is a false equation. At this point, perhaps an illustration will be helpful. It is 8:00 p.m. and I have the desire for a cup of coffee. How do I account for this desire? The contributing causes for this desire are numerous. I live in a coffee-drinking culture and was raised in a family of coffee drinkers. Many of the social interactions I enjoy are around a cup of coffee and I find the taste of coffee pleasurable. In fact, the taste is so pleasurable that after so many years of drinking coffee I have become psychologically dependent upon it, if not addicted. Further, the Dunkin Donuts advertisement informs me that, "America runs on coffee." Given all of these factors, how can I believe that this desire generated from within me? It would seem that Arthur Schopenhauer is right: "A man can do what he wants, but the catch is that he cannot will what he wills" (Katen, 314). Is there any place for a free will choice in this circumstance?

Compatibilism allows for the concession that my desire for coffee is not the result of a choice. The desire is the effect of the aforementioned causes. Nevertheless, in the context of this situation I can choose to have or not have the coffee. If I choose to have the coffee I will be responsible for not being able to fall asleep tonight and any subsequent dysfunctionality owing to sleep deprivation. I am not like a ping-pong ball going over Niagara Falls; I can choose to resist this desire and actualize my choice. An allegory that reinforces this idea is "Autobiography in Five Short Chapters," used in addiction recovery.

I

I walk down the street.
There is a deep hole in the sidewalk.
I fall in.
I am lost ... I am helpless.
It isn't my fault.
It takes forever to find a way out.

II

I walk down the street.
There is a deep hole in the sidewalk.
I pretend I don't see it.
I fall in again.
I can't believe I'm in the same place.
But, it isn't my fault.
It still takes a long time to get out.

III

I walk down the street.
There is a deep hole in the sidewalk.
I see it is there.
I still fall in ...it's a habit ... but,
my eyes are open.
I know where I am.
It is my fault.

I get out immediately.

IV

I walk down the same street.
There is a deep hole in the sidewalk.
I walk around it.

V

I walk down another street.

- Anonymous

According to compatibilism, *God's foreknowledge equals no free will* is another false equation. It is a non sequitur that God's knowledge of all things future constitutes coercion of all human beings to act in accordance with this foreknowledge. To believe foreknowledge negates free will is analogous to believing that knowledge of how a movie will end, because it is being seen for the second time, determines how the movie will end. It could be argued that God's knowledge of how people will use their free will has been integrated into the divine plan. Such incorporation does not imply hard determinism. For example, included in the New Testament is a narrative describing Pontius Pilate's decision to have Jesus of Nazareth executed by crucifixion. If this is what Pilate wanted to do, and apparently he did, then he exercised free will. He cannot be commended for his contribution to the plan of salvation. Rather, he is responsible for the execution of an innocent man and God is responsible for integrating Pilate's unjust sentence into the redemptive plan. A more ordinary illustration of non-coercive foreknowledge is accurately predicting that an honest man will tell the truth in a given situation. Knowing that a man will tell the truth is not tantamount to compelling him to speak truthfully.

There might be those who would view Pilate's placement in history as a form of *entrapment*. Legally, entrapment is the construction of a situation to induce a person to commit a crime that person would not have committed otherwise. Entrapment is illegal because it places someone who has no predisposition to commit a crime in a situation which any normal, law-abiding citizen would find irresistible. Ruling on the matter of entrapment, the Supreme Court's decision stated:

> To determine whether or not entrapment has been established, a line must be drawn between the trap for the unwary innocent and the trap for the unwary criminal (Sherman v. United States).

Implicit in this ruling is that a constructed situation that would *not* induce a normal, law-abiding citizen to commit a crime is not entrapment. This category of situation is referred to colloquially as a *sting*. A sting is within the law because the determining factor for the criminal act resides in the psychological state of the individual, not the orchestrated situation. Walter Stace addressed this difference in his essay on free will:

> ... free acts are all caused by desires, or motives, or by some sort of internal psychological states of the agent's mind. The unfree acts, on the other hand, are all caused by physical forces or physical conditions, outside the agent (Fineberg and Shafer-Landeau, 2002, 490).

Returning to Pilate's decision, it could be said that he was caught in a sting because his action was caused by his desire to do what was expedient – even if it meant the execution of an innocent man. Referring to Jesus, Pilate said: "I find no basis for a charge against him" (John 19:6, *New*

International Version) and, "I have found in him no grounds for the death penalty" (Luke 23:22, *New International Version*).

Conclusion

The Irish poet and dramatist Oscar Wilde is credited with having defined a dilemma as a situation in which no matter which of two options you choose, you will be wrong. Conversely, an *antinomy* is a situation in which no matter which of two options you choose, you will be right. An antinomy is, "the existence of two incompatible statements, each of which taken on its own, is reasonable" (Pence, 3). Rene Descartes classified the free will – determinism debate as an antinomy (Grim, 131).

A Hebrew Bible historical book, I Kings, records the wise ruling of Solomon when confronted by two women claiming the same infant son. The king was unable to discern which of the two women was the rightful mother until he called for a sword to have the baby cut in half and then divided between the disputing women. The case was settled when the actual mother said, "Please my lord, give her the living baby! Don't kill him!" The other woman said, "Neither I nor you shall have him. Cut him in two!" (I Kings 3:26) If the baby had been divided by the sword, both women would have lost, including the one who was telling the truth. In contrast to the case before Solomon, both sides in the free will – determinism debate are telling the truth. In the free will problem there is no "true mother" to be discerned.

The benefit of compatibilism is that both free will and determinism enjoy the status of being right. Imagine a world in which human beings were not responsible for their behavior. The fact that such a world has never existed is ample evidence that free will is right and necessary. Imagine a world in which the law of cause-and-effect did not apply. Certainly, it is not the world in which we live or anyone has ever lived. If either free will or determinism were *not* true, it would be impossible for people to manage their lives.

A compromise is required when opposing sides have equal and competing claims. People who say, "I never compromise when I am right," are properly asked, "When do you compromise, when you are wrong? Why should anyone compromise with you when you are wrong?" A compromise is a settlement of differences between two parties who are right, each in their own way. A compromise provides a solution in which the merits of both positions are retained. The free will - determinism problem is not like a Rubik's cube with a solution by which all sides are neatly reconciled. Neither is the free will problem like the case decided by Solomon, in which one claimant lost and the other won. The free will - determinism dispute is an antinomy that calls for each side to concede to the correctness of the other. Compatibilism includes these concessions. Compatibilism also requires each side to see itself, if standing alone, as an incomplete explanation of the human condition.

wicked; malevolent; sinful" (*American Heritage Dictionary*, 1969, 455). This apt description of Kuklinski raises the question of whether he was born evil or made this way. If he was not born evil it follows that he was nurtured into this objectionable state. In his interview with forensic psychiatrist Park Dietz, Kuklinski asked how he became a psychopath. Dr. Deitz's explanation included both nature and nurture. He explained to Kuklinski that he inherited his father's antisocial personality disorder which was exacerbated by the unspeakable physical abuse he experienced throughout his childhood.

The word "evil" appears 127 times in the New Testament and most often it is the Greek word *poneros* that is translated as "evil." (Greek is the original language of the New Testament.) *Poneros* is defined as "deliberate defiance of the moral law without regard to the pain and suffering brought to others by such defiance" (Thayer, 1996). Not all evil is deliberate *poneros*. There is a type of evil that could be characterized as ordinary since it is accomplished beneath the threshold of the evildoer's awareness. Edmund Burke posited, "The only thing necessary for the triumph of evil is for good men to do nothing" (2012). Adam Morton expresses a similar thought in the introduction of his book, *On Evil*: "When we think of evil we think first of large scale horrors. ... By the end of the book I hope to have convinced you that most evil acts are performed by people disturbingly like you and me" (2004, x).

Theologian S. Paul Schilling is slightly more specific with his assessment that often evil is enabled by a society in which its citizens are preoccupied with their mundane affairs:

> Without doubt, one of the greatest evils of all is the indifference to evil that characterizes enormous numbers of people who do not want to be disturbed as they pursue their parochial interests (1977, 21)

4. How Are We to Understand Human Evil?

I am what I am, and the truth is I don't give a flying (expletive delete) what anyone thinks of me.

\- Richard Kuklinski

Everyone in his own environment must strive to practice true humanity toward others. The future of the world depends on it.

\- Albert Schweitzer

The words of Richard Kuklinski, quoted above, are remarkable given that he killed over 250 people, the first when he was 13 years-old. Known as "The Ice Man," Kuklinski was a mafia contract killer for over four decades. If he is not an embodiment of human evil then one does not exist. In stark contrast to Kuklinski is Albert Schweitzer, also quoted above, who left a life of privilege to serve as a medical missionary in Africa for over half a century. Behaviorally these men are polar opposites; most lives are characterized between the extremes of malevolence and altruism. Still, it is a curiosity that the species that includes Richard Kuklinski also contains Albert Schweitzer. Hence this question: How are we to understand human evil?

What Is Evil?

Evil is distinct from natural disasters; there is no moral component to a flood, hurricane, tsunami, volcanic eruption or earthquake. To be precise, the phrase *human evil* is a redundancy. Evil is defined as, "morally bad or wrong;

If this analysis has a ring of familiarity it might be because Charles Dickens expressed it through Jacob Marley in *A Christmas Carol*. In his visitation to Ebenezer Scrooge, the deceased and condemned Marley warns Scrooge to take heed of the suffering around him:

> **Scrooge**: You always were a good man of business.
>
> **Marley**: Mankind was my business. The common good was my business. ...I walked through crowds of my fellow creatures with my eyes downwards. If but my eyes had been lead to see the misery around me, which was in my power to remove. But like yours Scrooge, these eyes saw nothing (2011, 16).

Also, evil is *ordinary* when people not usually associated with moral indifference act in such a way as to bring pain and suffering to others. The best known experimental instance of such behavior is Stanley Milgram's *Obedience and Compliance Experiment* (1974). Milgram hypothesized that people will not knowingly and willingly inflict pain on other people unless provoked in some extraordinary way. (Individuals who are psychopathic would be an exception.) As virtually every psychology student knows, Milgram hugely overestimated human decency. Sixty-percent of the participants who believed they were administering electrical shocks to other participants did so to the maximum voltage. (The shocks were not real and the recipients feigned pain by crying out for the experiment to stop.)

Nine years after Milgram's experiment, Philip Zombardo's *Stanford Prison Experiment* sustained Milgram's disheartening findings (1972). If the subjects in these experiments had been drawn from penitentiaries or psychiatric institutes the results would have been much less disturbing. In fact, Milgram's participants were respondents to a newspaper advertisement and Zimbardo's were twenty-four college students, thoroughly screened for mental and emotional stability.

While these two studies demonstrate ordinary people consciously behaving maliciously, Richard Rubenstien's investigation of the Holocaust revealed an evil accomplished with many of the perpetrators unaware. In *The Cunning of History*, he analyzes this genocide as the result of a carefully constructed division of labor in which many of its participants were oblivious to the finished product: a dead Jew. Rubenstein describes the unwitting cooperation of Jewish community councils (Judenrate) with the German SS in gathering those who eventually populated the concentration camps:

> In almost all the killing operations the German personnel were short-handed. It is estimated only fifty SS personnel and 200 Lett and Ukranian auxiliaries were assigned to the Warsaw Ghetto which had a population of five-hundred thousand at its peak, almost all of whom perished (1987, 74-75).

The astounding murder of Kitty Genovese supports Edmund Burke's observation that the passivity of good men facilitates the triumph of evil. On March 13, 1964 twenty-nine year-old Kitty Genovese was attacked in a Queens, New York parking lot and stabbed to death by her assailant, Winston Moseley. A disturbing feature of this homicide is that at least a dozen (and perhaps as many as thirty-eight) residents of a nearby apartment building heard her cries for help. To this day, social psychologists use this murder to illustrate two phenomena of noninvolvement: the *bystander effect* and *diffusion of responsibility*.

Sociologist Samuel Oliner has a personal interest in explaining why some people are *bystanders* and others intervene to assist those in harm's way. (Oliner refers to those who help as rescuers.) His experience as a Holocaust survivor provoked his curiosity about a Gentile (non-Jewish) family that took him in and protected him from abduction by the Gestapo. In so doing, they risked their own lives. His determination to understand this family's altruism, especially that of its matriarch, Balwina Piecuch, has energized him for over two decades of research.

> Balwina Piecuch's acts of kindenss and caring not only served my life, it formed my life. I emigrated to the United States, became a sociologist, and spent my career working to understand what motivates altruists like Balwina and the hundreds of thousands of people who put the welfare of others alongside their own (Oliner, 2001).

The renown psychiatrist and author Scott Peck believed the phenomenon of human goodness is more mysterious than human depravity. *In The People of the Lie: The Hope for Healing Human Evil* he posited:

> The problem of evil can hardly be separated from the problem of goodness. Were there no goodness in the world, we would not even be considering the problem of evil. ... we automatically assume this is a naturally good world that has somehow been contaminated by evil. In terms of what we know of science, however, it is actually easier to explain evil. ... That children generally lie and cheat and steal is routinely observable. The fact that sometimes they grow up to become truly honest adults is what seems the more remarkable. ... If we seriously think about it, it probably makes more sense to assume this is a naturally evil world that has somehow been mysteriously "contaminated" by goodness, rather

> than the other way around. The mystery of goodness is even greater than the mystery of evil (1998, 41).

Circumstantial Evil

Psychology's *fundamental attribution error* teaches that it is erroneous to attribute an individual's behavior to personality without also considering the influence of the situation that provided the context for the behavior. For instance, to equate Chris Kyle, who has killed 160 people, with the aforementioned Richard Kuklinski without considering that Kyle is a Navy Seal sniper whose killing took place in Operation Iraqi Freedom would constitute the *fundamental attribution error*.

Two stunning occurrences of evil that arose from circumstances amply demonstrate that nature and nurture by themselves are insufficient to account for conduct unbecoming a human being in some situations. On March 16, 1968 American soldiers in Vietnam entered the village of My Lai and killed at least 347 and possibly 504 unarmed Vietnamese civilians, many of them women or children. Twenty-six soldiers from Charlie Company were charged with criminal offenses for their actions at My Lai with only one, Lieutenant William Calley, being convicted and imprisoned. Peck, who chaired a committee of three psychiatrists that investigated the massacre at My Lai, attributed it to a confluence of circumstances. One of his conclusions is that *group evil* exceeds *individual evil* in severity because it disperses responsibility and provides a cloak of anonymity for the perpetrators.

Prior to the September 11, 2001 attack on the World Trade Center the single greatest loss of American civilian life occurred on November 18, 1978 in the mass suicide of a transplanted religious community. In 1974 Reverend James Jones relocated his San Franciso congregation, the People's

Temple, to Jonestown, Guyana on the northern coast of South America. Fearing an imminent congressional investigation would lead to the dissolution of the community, Jones and 909 of his followers committed suicide by drinking flavored water mixed with cyanide. While there is no disputing that Jones is a striking example of individual evil, this mass suicide is also an instantiation of group evil since 200 children, many of them infants, were given the lethal drink by their parents. The People's Temple being a closed community, many miles from its California roots, and led by a charismatic minister combined for the perfect storm that culminated in this tragedy.

Pathological Evil

The ease with which a list of appalling, premeditated evil acts is composed is indeed troubling. Equally disturbing is the frequency with which child abductions, child abuse, serial murders, and Ponzi schemes are reported in the news. The July 29, 2010 cover of *Time* magazine shows an eighteen year-old Afghani woman without a nose, her mutilation (which also included the removal of her ears) resulted from the ruling of a Taliban commander. This was her punishment for running away from her abusive husband and in-laws. In 1970 social workers discovered a thirteen year-old girl who had lived in social isolation for most of her life. Alone day after day, strapped to a potty chair, "Genie" (case study name) spent eleven years in a barely furnished room with undecorated walls.

Whatever their differences, serial murderers Ted Bundy, Jeffrey Dahmer, John Wayne Gacy, and Edmund Kemper share a psychiatric designation: psychopath. Premeditated murder accomplished without conscience is psychopathological evil. Robert Hare, an internationally recognized expert on psychopathic behavior and author of

Without Conscience: The Disturbing World of Psychopaths Among Us, begins his book with an unsettling narrative:

> Several years ago two graduate students and I submitted a paper to a scientific journal. The paper described an experiment in which we had used a biochemical recorder to monitor electrical activity in the brains of several groups of adult men while they performed a language task. This activity was traced on chart paper as a series of waves, referred to as an electroenchephalogram (EEG). The editor returned the paper with his apologies. His reason, he told us, "Frankly, we found some of the brain wave patterns depicted in the paper very odd. Those EEG's couldn't have come from real people."
>
> Some of the brain wave patterns were indeed odd, but we hadn't gathered them from aliens and we certainly hadn't made them up. We had obtained them from a class of individuals found in every race, culture, society, and walk of life. Everybody has met these people, been deceived and manipulated by them, and forced to live or repair the damage they have wrought. These often charming – but often deadly – individuals have a clinical name: *psychopaths* (1993, 1).

The psychotic murderous activities of Peter Carlquist, a man with paranoid schizophrenia, and Andrea Yates, a profoundly depressed woman who suffered with auditory hallucinations, are no less abhorrent than those of serial murderers. Whether it is done without conscience or without an appreciation of what is being done, murder is psychopathological evil.

Conclusion

Manifestations of evil are several. This chapter expresses an effort to be more specific in discussing malevolent human behavior by distinguishing several subcategories: ordinary evil, circumstantial evil, psychopathic evil, and psychotic evil. What is not accomplished in this piece, or even attempted, is a comprehensive explanation of why evil occurs. Such an explanation is beyond the capability and scope of this or any other treatise on the subject.

The question, *Are human beings by nature good or evil?* will continue to be debated into the foreseeable future. In one such debate, the humanistic psychologist Carl Rogers affirmed that we are, by nature, good:

> Though I am very well aware of the incredible amount of destructive, cruel, malevolent behavior in today's world from the threats of war to the senseless violence in the streets – I do not find this evil is inherent in human nature... my experience leads me to believe that it is cultural influences which are the major factor in our evil behaviors. The rough manner of childbirth; the infant's mixed experience with the parents; the constricting, destructive influence of our educational system; the injustice of our distribution of wealth; our cultivated prejudices against individuals who are different – all these elements and many others warp the human organism in directions which are antisocial. So I see members of the human species, like members of other species, as essentially constructive in their fundamental nature, but damaged by their experience (1981).

Psychiatrist Rollo May countered that Rogers and those agreeing with him have overestimated the corrupting influence of society:

Culture admittedly has powerful effects upon us. But it could not have these effects were these tendencies not already present in us. Who makes up the culture except persons like you and me? The culture is evil as well as good because we, the human beings who constitute it, are evil as well as good. ... Some people who join and lead the humanistic movement do so in order to find a haven, a port in the storm, a community of like-minded persons who are also playing possum to the evils about us. Life to me, is not a requirement to live out a preordained pattern of goodness, but a challenge coming down through the centuries out of the fact that each of us can throw the lever toward good or evil (1982).

5. Are There Universal Virtues?

Two things fill the mind with ever new and increasing awe: the stars above me and the moral law within me.

- Immanuel Kant

Assume a virtue if you have it not.

- Hamlet, Act 3, Scene 4

Well-known among psychologists is Gordon Allport's study of human traits in which he enumerated 17,953 words in the English language that describe a personality characteristic (1936). Of course, not all of these attributes are praiseworthy as virtues. Areteology is the study of virtue, derived from the Greek word *arete* which means excellence. Simply stated, virtue is moral excellence, goodness, righteousness. Philosopher Mike W. Martin has written:

> Theories of virtue are grounded in theories about human nature, that is, theories about what it means to be a human being. Human nature is described in terms of the capacities, problems, possibilities, and aspirations of people. Virtues are then defined as character traits that enable people to achieve the good that is possible for them (1989, 37).

Are there universal virtues? The issue this question implies can be stated as follows:

> Plato and Aristotle, the two great Greek ethicists inspired by Socrates, base their theories of human nature on a key assumption. They assume that reasoning is the primary purpose or function that sets

> human beings apart from other creatures. In their view, virtues are the excellences that enable humans to exercise their powers of reasoning and live in accordance with their conclusions. Hence, in living the virtuous life, one lives well that distinctive form of life possible for humans (Martin, 1989, 37).

Is there something inherent in human beings that compels us to esteem certain characteristics as excellent – traits we admire in others and desire for ourselves? If so, this would imply there are qualities that all people from all eras have endorsed as exemplary. A study published in 2004 provided data that affirms this to be the case.

Psychologists Martin Seligman and Chris Peterson found six traits transculturally recognized as virtues across human history. In *Authentic Happiness*, Seligman described their methodology:

> We read Aristotle and Plato, Aquinas and Augustine, the Old Testament and the Talmud, Confucius, Buddha, Lao-Tze, Bushido (the samurai code), the Koran, Benjamin Franklin, and the Upanishads – some two-hundred virtue catalogs in all. To our surprise, almost every one of these traditions flung across three-thousand years and the entire face of the earth endorsed six virtues: wisdom and knowledge, courage, love and humanity, justice, temperance, spirituality and transcendence (2002, 132-133).

Western philosophy has long referred to four virtues as fundamental: courage, self-control, justice, and wisdom. Plato wrote of them in the fourth century B.C. and seven centuries later Saint Ambrose designated them the four cardinal virtues. This agreement between ancient philosophy and contemporary psychology make reasonable the claim that universal virtues exist. Seligman and Peterson coined the term ubiquitous virtues to designate the virtues they discovered from their research.

The balance of this chapter addresses the implication of the existence of virtues that cultures across time and place have considered commendable. Questions considered are: What benefits derive from moral uprightness? Is an individual's life enriched by virtuous conduct or is it only society that benefits? Can moral excellence be nurtured?

The Benefits of Moral Uprightness

To be free of guilt or responsibility is indeed a benefit. Shakespeare wrote, "a still and quiet conscience (is) a peace above all earthly dignities" (King Henry VIII, Act 3, Scene 2). Clearly, this serenity is not available to the Reverend Arthur Dimmesdale, a character in Nathaniel Hawthorne's novel, The Scarlet Letter. Set in Puritan New England, it is the story of Hester Prynne, whose extramarital affair results in an illegitimate child and community scorn. Taking responsibility for her sin, she carries herself with dignity, raising her child and never revealing Dimmesdale as the father. His inauthentic life remained unknown to all, except himself and Hester. He lives out his years tormented by the duplicity of being an adulterer while maintaining his position as the community's respected spiritual leader.

> It is the unspeakable misery of a life so false as his, that it steals the pith and substance out of whatever realities there are around us, and which were meant by Heaven to be the spirit's joy and nutriment. To the untrue man, the whole universe is false – it is impalpable – it shrinks to nothing within his grasp. And he himself, in so far as he shows himself in a

> false light, becomes a shadow, or indeed, ceases to exist (1978, 107).

In addition to the peace of mind an unburdened conscience provides for individuals, a social benefit is derives from their adherence to moral excellence.

Evolutionary psychology is the study of mind and behavior using the principles of natural selection. It posits the behaviors that contribute to the survival and perpetuation of the human species are encoded in all people to ensure the continuation of humankind. (Sociopaths being a noteworthy exception.) Conscience is the inner feeling or voice that provides the awareness of a moral aspect to one's conduct. Imagine the consequences if all human beings had neither an ethical code nor a moral compass. Imagine a society in which all members behave unconscionably, with no regard for the virtues of self-restraint, justice, charity or courage. Such a society could not endure. Courageous hunters feed tribes, self-sacrificing parents nurture children, honest judges administer justice, and wise leaders prepare for the future. The benefits of the ubiquitous virtues extend well beyond an individual's untroubled conscience.

Can Moral Excellence Be Nurtured?

Thomas Lickona has committed his professional life to character education - the moral development of children. The introduction to his book, Character Matters, includes:

> Many of us are now coming to recognize ... that it is not possible to develop a virtuous society unless we develop virtue in the hearts, minds, and souls of individual human beings. Families, schools, and communities can and must each do their part in creating a culture of character by raising children of

> character. Indeed, the health of our nation in the century ahead depends on how seriously all of us commit to this calling (2004, xxvi).

Professor Lickona is not alone with this conviction. Over the last forty years, Robert Coles, Daniel Goleman, William Kirk Kilpatrick, Stanley Milgram, Samuel Oliner, and Philip Zombardo have contributed to a body of literature supporting Martin Luther King, Jr.'s assertion: "Intelligence plus character – that is the goal of true education (Lickona, 2004, xi).

Nevertheless, it is logical to ask: If virtuous behavior is innate, as evolutionary psychology implies, then why does it have to be taught? The answer lies in the composition of human beings. We have the ability to reason how we ought to behave in order to effect our own good and the good of others. But we also have passions that often compete with reason and move us to behave contrary to the best interests of ourselves and others. When this conflict occurs, it is the conscience that draws upon our knowledge and experience to inform us of the possible undesirable consequences of dissolute behavior, disrupting the "clear and quiet conscience" of which Shakespeare wrote. The human predicament includes the ongoing challenge to conform our behavior to the virtues we espouse. The Apostle Paul confessed to his engagement in this struggle in his letter to the Romans: "I do not understand what I do. For what I want to do I do not do, but what I hate I do" (Romans 7:15, NIV). What is innate are the capacities to recognize the ubiquitous virtues as praiseworthy and learn good character. A virtuous life is effected by choice, not forced by instinct.

In Ethical Wisdom: What Makes Us Good, journalist Mark Matousek amplifies Immanuel Kant's suggestion of a relationship between the starry heavens above him and his conscience within:

Zoroastrians believe that gravity, the force drawing planets together in space, is love itself. John Dewey, of library fame, came to an oddly similar conclusion. The father of the Dewey decimal system was apparently a closet mystic: "The spiritual life gets its surest and most ample guarantees when it is learned that the laws and conditions of righteousness are implicated in the working processes of the universe; when it is found that man in his conscious struggles, in his doubts, temptations and defeats, in his aspirations and successes, is moved on and buoyed up by the forces which have developed nature." When we look at ourselves this way, as upcroppings of nature obeying harmonious laws, something beams inside the brain. Our moral sense is sharpened and heightened, elevated by something greater (Matousek, 2011, 225).

6. Why Are Some People Extraordinarily Resilient and Why Do Other People Opt Out of Life?

Was mich nicht umbringt, macht mich starker.
(That which does not kill me, makes me stronger.)
- Friedrich Nietzsche

Although the world is full of suffering, it is also full of overcoming it.
- Helen Keller

A 1981 *Sports Illustrated* story written by Frank Deford entitled "Kenny, Dying Young" recounts the story of Kenny Wright, a high school football star who committed suicide after a spinal cord injury left him a quadriplegic (Deford, 1981). Three years earlier, another football star, Darryl Stingley of the New England Patriots, suffered a similar injury. In a pre-season game against the Oakland Raiders, a collision on the field resulted in a spinal cord injury and life as a quadriplegic. Stingley did not commit suicide. Instead, he finished his college degree, continued parenting three sons, worked in the front office of the Patriots, and started a not-for-profit organization for at-risk youths in his hometown Chicago. Five years after his injury, he wrote a memoir, *Happy to Be Alive* (1983).

Another magazine story, this one with the title, "A Deadly Struggle Against the Sea," describes Janet Culver's fourteen day battle to survive after a sailboating accident (Culver, 1989). Adrift on a life raft with her sailing partner, Nicholas Abbot, on the tenth day he withdrew from the struggle to survive by drowning himself. Janet Culver survived to tell her story.

What accounts for Darryl Stingley's resilience and Kenny Wright's suicide? What enabled Janet Culver to persevere in the same situation that drove Nicholas Abbot to despair and self-determined death? In the preface to a collection of essays on suicide published a few years ago, the editor expressed his long running curiosity about why people commit suicide:

> A wise and helpful professor once advised me to locate the "fire that burns within" for the topic of my doctoral dissertation. He reasoned that since I would be immersed in the topic for several years, it should be one that would sustain my interest. I opted for suicide and, fifteen years after the completion of my dissertation, I confess to giving disproportionate attention to suicide in the courses I teach as well as gravitating toward suicidal patients in my clinical work. Why? Perhaps Camus is right: "There is but one truly serious philosophical problem, and that is suicide. Judging whether life is or is not worth living amounts to answering the fundamental question of philosophy" (Malikow, 2009, xi).

Why are some people extraordinarily persistent and why do other people opt out of life? As with so many questions concerning human behavior, the variables of personality and perception preclude an uncomplicated answer. Persistence is the quality of continuing in a course of action in spite of discouragement, opposition, and/or failure. Perseverance, the determination to remain constant in purpose, is synonymous with persistence. Resilience, the capacity to return to a previous condition or regain a high level of functioning following a loss, is an expression of persistence. Consider the descriptions of two men and guess which one persevered in life and which one committed suicide:

In 1973 D.C. was severely burned in an automobile explosion. In the accident he lost two-thirds of his skin, both hands, both eyes, and both ears. In addition to disfigurement, D.C. was facing a lifetime of medical procedures and intense, unremitting pain. D.W. wrote a novel that was included on *Time* magazine's list of the "100 Best Novels" written between 1923 and 2003. A brilliant, popular college professor and multiple award winning author, as a teenager he was a nationally ranked junior tennis player.

Given the context of these descriptions, likely you chose D.W. as the one who committed suicide and D.C. as the one who persevered. If you did, you chose correctly. However, even if you guessed correctly, didn't it seem counter-intuitive? D.C. is Dax Cowart, who wanted to die following his accident and for a time appealed to have his medical treatment discontinued. Yet, eventually, he accepted his lot as "The Man Sentenced to Life," graduated from law school, and married (Wicker, 1989). His legal specialty is medical ethics and patients' rights. D.W. is David Foster Wallace, whose suicide in 2008 at the age of 46 deprived the literary world of an extraordinary talent. Wallace had suffered from a near lifelong depression that eventually resisted treatment, including psychotherapy, antidepressant medications, and ECT (electroconvulsive therapy). A complete understanding of Cowart's resilience and Wallace's suicide is an impossibility. Nevertheless, from an analysis of a number of instances of people who have persevered and those who did not, a partial understanding is attainable.

Examples of Perseverance

H. Jackson Brown, author of the bestseller, *Life's Little Instruction Book*, has provided a picturesque description of perseverance: "In the confrontation between the stream and the rock, the stream always wins – not through strength but by perseverance" (2012). The renown existentialist Albert Camus discovered his own resilience and described it with these words: "In the midst of winter, I finally learned there was in me an invincible summer" (2011). Impressive instances of perseverance and resilience are not difficult to find. Here are a few:

> Paul Wittgenstien resumed his career as a concert pianist after having his right arm amputated during World War I.
>
> Ludwig von Beethoven began to lose his hearing at age 26 and was totally deaf by age 44, resulting in a career change from pianist to composer.
>
> Elyn Saks is a professor at the University of Southern California School of Law and on the psychiatry faculty of the University of California School of Medicine. She graduated valedictorian from Vanderbilt University, studied at Oxford, and earned her law degree at Yale University. Her bestselling memoir, *The Center Cannot Hold: My Journey Through Madness*, recounts her life with schizophrenia, the condition that manifested when she was eight years-old.
>
> Michael J. Fox has continued his distinguished acting career after being diagnosed with Parkinson's disease at age thirty. He is the founder of a foundation for Parkinson's research.

Examples of Surrender

As well, instances of giving up when challenged are easily found. In November of 1980 the phrase "No mas!" was immortalized in boxing history when one of the sport's greatest champions, Roberto Duran, quit in the eighth round of his fight with Sugar Ray Leonard. ("No mas" is Spanish, translated as, "no more.") Far more serious than withdrawing from a boxing match is deciding "no mas" to life. The esteemed psychologist Lawrence Kohlberg, suffering with an incurable disease, made this decision in 1987 at age 60. Another well-known psychologist, Bruno Bettelheim, a Holocaust survivor, also committed suicide. Like David Foster Wallace, he had suffered most of his life with depression.

Psychologist Kay Jamison's investigation of the occurrence of mood disorders among artistic geniuses generated an impressive list of celebrated artists who chose to end their lives. Poets Sylvia Plath and Anne Sexton, novelists Virginia Woolf, Hunter Thompson, and Lucy Maude Montgomery, and painters Vincent van Gogh and Alberto Greco are among the creative artists who committed suicide. Jamison, an accomplished writer herself, once attempted suicide when suffering extreme depression from bipolar disorder. In *Touched with Fire: Manic-Depressive Illness and the Artistic Temperament* she presents the case for, " ... the importance of moods in igniting thought, changing perceptions, creating chaos, forcing order upon that chaos, and enabling transformation" (1996, 6). In her estimation, the wide ranging, intense moods that fuel creativity also induce suicidality. Similarly, Edwin Sheidman's research revealed an overrepresentation of suicide among people with I.Q.'s in the genius category (1998). Such findings are consistent with the biblical observation, "With much wisdom comes much sorrow; the more knowledge, the more grief" (Ecclesiastes 1:18).

A shocking instance of giving up on life was reported in a recent Newsweek magazine story concerning veterans of the wars in Afghanistan and Iraq:

> About 18 veterans kill themselves each day. Thousands from the current wars have already done so. In fact, the number of U.S. Soldiers who have died by their own hand is now estimated to be greatert than the number (6,460) who have died in combat in Afghanistan and Iraq (Swofford, 2012, 29, 30).

Towards an Understanding

How is the difference in resilience between Darryl Stingley and Kenny Wright explained or the difference in persistence between Janet Culver and Nicholas Abbot understood? A comprehensive accounting for these differences is impossible because all of the factors that contribute to an individual's traits cannot be known. *Personality* is the aggregate of those traits; it is "an individual's characteristic pattern of thinking, feeling, and acting" (Myers, 2007, 598). The contributions of nature and nurture and their interaction with a continuously changing environment forbid a complete explanation of why some people are more persistent than others. Although the impossibility of a complete explanation must be granted, a partial understanding is attainable. Towards that end, two conditions that develop persistence will be considered, followed by three contributors to succumbing.

Understanding Persistence

Shortly after graduating from college, Francesco Clark dived into a swimming pool and suffered a spinal cord injury that left him a quadriplegic. In addition to the loss of the use of his arms and legs, he lost the ability to perspire, causing an extremely irritating skin condition. Without formal training in either chemistry or dermatology, Clark developed a lotion to treat his condition. Eventually, this led to the founding of Clark's Botanicals, an international producer and distributor of cosmetic products.

Richard Cohen is a nationally syndicated columnist and four time Pulitizer Prize recipient. In addition, he is nearly blind, twice a cancer survivor, and limited by multiplesclerosis. In his memoir, *Blindsided: Living a Life Above Illness - A Reluctant Memoir*, he shares a daily conversation he has with himself, lest he despair over his continually deteriorating body:

> I feel weak because I acknowledge the realities of my life. We exist in a culture that celebrates strength. Men are strong and self-reliant. I am weakened and need the help of others. There is no escape from the rust I see on my body.
>
> I must rise above the culture of perfection and remember that I can be even if I can no longer do. I am learning to acknowledge weakness, accept assistance, and discover new forms of self-definition. My formula has changed. I do not read self-absorbed men's magazines or go to Vin Diesel movies. A new male idea will have to do. I cannot allow myself to be held captive by old dreams.
>
> Success comes today by a different standard, measured by more cerebral achievements and often centered on the lives of my children. ... Dealing with challenges to health is a great ally in nurturing that change in priorities (2004, 22).

What accounts for the resilience of Francesco Clark and perseverance of Richard Cohen? One factor is their ability and willingness to reframe their circumstances without denying reality. By constructing different, but nonetheless accurate, descriptions of their situations they have been able to redirect themselves and adapt. Rather than lamenting the loss of their well-functioning bodies, Clark and Cohen have redefined their lives by choosing to focus on new priorities. For Clark this meant abandoning his dream of a career in the fashion magazine industry; for Cohen it meant the importance once placed on physical fitness (jogging and tennis) be reassigned to family and writing. *Framing* is the psychological term for what these men are accomplishing.

> Although it is not a part of clinical jargon, framing is an essential concept in psychotherapy, referring to *how we choose to describe a situation*. Framing refers to how we feel about and understand our circumstances and largely determines whether or not we will find a reason to be grateful, regardless of the conditions in which we find ourselves (Malikow, 2010, 61).

In addition to the capacity to reframe, resilience is strengthened by a sense of responsibility. The German existentialist Friedrich Nietzsche wrote: "He who has a why to live for can bear with almost any how" (Frankl, 1959, 97). Psychiatrist Gordon Livingston employs this concept when working with suicidal patients:

> When confronted with a suicidal person I seldom try to talk them out of it. Instead I ask them to examine what it is that has so far dissuaded them from killing themselves. Usually this involves finding out what the connections are that tether that person to life in the face of nearly unbearable psychic pain (2004, 72).

A stunning confession by Abraham Lincoln made it clear that he suffered from nearly unbearable psychic pain:

> I am the most miserable man living. If what I feel were equally distributed to the whole human family, there would not be one cheerful face on earth. Whether I shall ever be better, I cannot tell; I awfully forebode I shall not. To remain as I am is impossible; I must die or be better, it appears to me (Shenk, 2005, 56).

Lincoln triumphed over his depression by not allowing it to prevent him from doing his duty. He believed, "he had been charged with so vast and sacred a trust that he felt he had no moral right to shrink from his responsibilities" (66).

> Although Lincoln's theology is not altogether clear, there is no mistaking that he carried on his work with a sense of calling; a determination to accomplish something while he lived; and to have his name connected "with the great events of his generation" (Malikow, 2008. 9).

Although few of us will have our names connected with the great events of our generation, we need the reassurance that our life has significance. "We need to know that we matter to the world, that the world takes us seriously" (Kushner, 2001, 5).

Understanding Suicide

Psychologist David Rudd has written of four central themes in a suicidal belief system:

> (1) unlovability ("I don't deserve to live"); (2) helplessness ("I can't solve my problems"); (3) poor

> distress tolerance or psychache ("I can't stand this pain anymore"); (4) perceived burdensomeness ("Everyone would be better off if I were dead") (Shneidman, 2004, 139).

According to his analysis, people who give up on life perceive themselves as unworthy to live, incapable of managing their problems, unable to continue suffering, and diluting the quality of life for others. Rudd's four themes are illustrated by the suicides cited earlier in this essay. Janet Culver described Nicholas Abbot as overwhelmed by guilt for his failure to adequately equip the sailboat for an emergency. Unable to forgive himself, he felt he didn't deserve to live. Lawrence Kohlberg and Kenny Wright were in despair over their helplessness to improve their irreversible conditions. In spite of his brilliance, David Foster Wallace was unable to find a way to relieve his psychache. And Kenny Wright concluded that he would be a lifelong burden to his devoted mother.

Psychiatrist John Maltsberger has offered two additional themes in a suicidal belief system: rage and aloneness (1987). Rage seems the best explanation for this shocking murder-suicide that occurred in Florida:

> On May 27, 2006 an Illinois physician threw his eight and four year-old sons from the fifteenth floor balcony of the hotel where they were vacationing. Dr. Edward Van Dyke then followed his sons over the railing by jumping to his own death (Malikow, 2008, 85).

Dr. Van Dyke did not leave a suicide note, making it more difficult to explain this tragedy. It is likely this hideous act was motivated by rage toward his wife for something she actually did or he imagined as part of a psychotic delusion.

In the *Nicomachean Ethics*, Aristotle reflects on the value of friendship: "Without friends, no one would choose to live though he had all other goods" (1999, VIII, 119). Stephen King's novella, *Rita Hayworth and Shawshank Redemption*, provides a dramatic example of a suicide driven by aloneness (1982). One of the characters, an elderly convict named Brooks Hatlen, is paroled after over fifty years of imprisonment. Although free, he is friendless and isolated in a world that terrifies him. Separated from the only community he has known for over half his life, Brooks Hatlen hanged himself from the ceiling beam in his boarding house room.

Conclusion

Lance Armstrong, a seven time Tour de France bicycle race winner and a cancer survivor, expresses his philosophy of pain and perseverance in his bestselling memoir:

> Pain is temporary. It may last a minute, or an hour, or a day, or a year, but eventually it will subside and something else will take its place. If I quit, however, it lasts forever. That surrender, even the smallest act of giving up, stays with me. So when I feel like quitting, I ask myself, which would I rather live with? ...By now you've figured out I'm into pain. Why? Because it's self-revelatory, that's why. There is a point in every race when a rider encounters his real opponent and understands that it's himself. In my most painful moments on the bike, I am at my most curious, and I wonder each and every time how I will respond. Will I discover my innermost weakness, or will I seek out my innermost strength? It's an open-ended question whether or not I will be able to finish the race. You might say pain is my chosen way of exploring the human heart (2000, 269-270).

What is the explanation for Armstrong's determination and pain tolerance? Why isn't everyone like him? Why are some people extraordinarily persistent, and why do other people opt out of life? Apart from the genetic contribution to personality, an individual's training, support, and models provide a partial answer to this question. Rudyard Kipling's classic poem, "If," includes this qualification for adulthood:

> If you can force your heart and nerve and sinew
> To serve your turn long after they are gone
> And so hold on when there is nothing left in you
> Except the will which says to them "hold on" (1910).

Few have held on as remarkably and resolutely as Bob Shumaker, held as a prisoner of war for eight years in North Vietnam including three years in solitary confinement. Reflecting on those years, he attributes his survival and resumption of a normal life to the support of his fellow POW's and mental discipline. No doubt the latter was nurtured by his training as a Navy officer and pilot. In an interview Shumaker offered this explanation.

> The worst thing I and my fellow POW's could have done under the circumstances would have been to clam up and withdraw. That would have been easy because our captors kept us in four by nine concrete windowless cells; they imposed a no communication policy on us. But we thwarted them by developing a tap code which allowed us to clandestinely communicate with our neighbors a foot away through a concrete wall using coded knocks that spelled out words. What did we talk about? It didn't really matter. We just knew that there was a fellow American sharing our experience. We built houses in our minds – tapped out French and music lessons, computed the

> 12th root of the number two, relived pleasant past relationships and even had elaborate breakfasts each Sunday (all in our imaginations). We were focused on supporting each other, trying to make life a bit more bearable, and dreaming (2010).

Today Shumaker lives in the house he mentally constructed board by board, nail by nail as a POW. (Of course, it has an open floor plan, plenty of windows, and minimal concrete.)

Resiliency also is required of those whose functioning has been impaired by disease or accident. Dr. Dennis Charney of the Mount Sinai School of Medicine believes, "Social support is essential to resilience" (2010). Occupational therapists work with patients to assist them in recovering daily living and work skills. Nancy Kelly, Supervisor of Occupational Therapy at Brigham and Women's Hospital in Boston, stresses the contribution of support to a patient's determination to survive and regain as much functionality as possible (2012). A family's love and encouragement combined with professional instruction on how to adapt to life following a spinal cord injury, stroke, amputation, or other misfortune expedites and augments resilience.

Child psychiatrist Robert Coles agrees with the adage, "Values are not taught, they are caught." His five decades of research on the moral development of children has brought him to this conclusion:

> "Moral intelligence" isn't acquired only by the memorization of rules and regulations, by dint of abstract classroom discussion or kitchen compliance. We grow morally as a consequence of learning how to be with others, how to behave in this world, a learning prompted by taking to heart what we have seen and

> heard. The child is a witness; the child is an ever-attentive witness of grown-up morality – or lack thereof; the child looks and looks for cues as to how one ought to behave, and finds them galore as we parents and teachers go about our lives, making choices, addressing people, showing in action our rock-bottom assumptions, desires, and values, and thereby telling those young observers much more than we may realize (1998, 5).

Coles, Daniel Goleman, William Kirk Kilpatrick, Richard Lavoie, Thomas Lickona and Samuel Oliner, all authorities on moral devlopment and character education, agree that the acquisition of values begins in childhood by direct observation. The values children internalize and carry into adulthood are the values their parents and significant other adults have consistently demonstrated. Among these values are persistence, perseverance, and resilience.

7. What Is the Place of Emotions in the Human Predicament?

But are not this struggle and even the mistakes one may make better, and do they not develop us more, than if we kept systematically away from emotions?

- Vincent van Gogh

Moods and metaphors are more apt to sway and persuade than mere logic and evidence. The heart is stirred by emotion, but chilled by an assault based on pure reason.

- Avery Weisman

I am a rock, I am an island. And a rock feels no pain, and an island never cries.

- Paul Simon

A common social greeting is, "How are you today?" Consider what would happen if this question were always received as a sincere inquiry as to our feelings and we carefully deliberated before responding. Our responses would not be a perfunctory, "Fine," or cursory, "O.K." Instead, a moment or more of introspection would precede the announcement of some emotional state. Emotions are so interlaced into our moment by moment experiences that they are as the water is to fish that swim unaware of their submergence. The American Psychiatric Association has designated certain feelings as abnormal and placed them in a distinct category - *affective disorders*, also referred to as *mood disorders*. A reading of the *Diagnostic and Statistical Manual* reveals that mental health professionals consider prolonged periods of sadness (depression) to be a pathological emotional condition. They believe the same about the inability to experience pleasure (anhedonia) and elevated mood and energy (*mania*).

A challenge confronting psychologists is understanding emotions; a challenge facing all human beings is managing them. The difficulty of this task was recognized long ago by Aristotle, who addressed the emotion of anger in his *Rhetoric*: "Anyone can become angry, that is easy. But to become angry with the right person, to the right degree, at the right time, for the right purpose is not within everybody's power and is not easy" (1954, II, 2). Similarly, the Hebrew Bible considers a man who controls his emotions more commendable than a man heroic in battle: "Better a patient man than a warrior, a man who controls his temper than one who takes a city" (Proverbs 16:32, *New International Version*).

The two questions that comprise this chapter are: (1) Given the difficulty of managing emotions and problems that result from the failure to do so, are feelings an asset or a liability of the human condition? (2) Since some emotions are unpleasant, would a life without feelings be preferable to a life with them?

What Are Emotions?

"Emotions are a response of the whole organism involving (1) physiological arousal, (2) expressive behaviors, and (3) conscious experience, including thoughts and feelings" (Myers, 2007, 514). The exact number of emotions available to human beings is unknown. Two frequently cited compilations have been provided by Robert Plutchik, a psychologist, and Aristotle, a philosopher. Plutchik postulated the existence of eight emotions: *fear, anger, sadness, joy, disgust, trust, anticipation, and surprise* (1980). Aristotle's list, although different, also consists of eight emotions: *anger, love, fear, shame, kindness, pity, indignation, and envy* (1954, II). Plutchik's list has an equal number of positive and negative emotions; Aristotle's shows a five to three division favoring negative emotions.

However, an evaluation of emotions as positive or negative requires the qualification that many emotions are two edged swords. Indeed, love is a many splendored thing, but the assessment that, " 'Tis better to have loved and lost than to have never loved at all" is debatable (Tennyson, 1850). Conversely, fear, an unpleasant emotion, is beneficial in that it alerts and protects, contributing to survival. Many who suffer with anxiety have resorted to anti-anxiety medications for relief and there is some evidence that anxiety contributes to peptic ulcers. However, neurobiologist Robert Sapolsky has posited that animals who lack the capacity for anxiety are more vulnerable to predators (2004, 319-321). Anger, although distasteful, can provide the energy for a salutary accomplishment. The anger of anticrime activist John Walsh led to the television program "America's Most Wanted," which has contributed to the capture of over 1,000 fugitives. (Walsh's six year-old son, Adam, was abducted and murdered in 1981.)

Emotions: A Cost-Benefit Analysis

The science fiction classic, "The Terminator," features a cyborg, dispatched to kill the movie's heroine, Sarah Conner. The high-tech killing machine is described to her with these words: "That thing is out there. It can't be bargained with; it can't be reasoned with; it doesn't feel pain or pity or remorse. And it will not stop until you are dead!" (1984). Unencumbered by feelings, the "Terminator" engages in its mission with inhuman and inhumane efficiency.

In the spirit of science fiction, consider the possibility of *affective neutralization* brain surgery. If you opt for it, post-operatively, you would live the rest of your life devoid of feelings. Would you agree to this hypothetical procedure that would render you *emotionless*? Do you consider this condition an existential upgrade? A patient well-known among neuroscientists, referred to as Elliot, is a real-life instantiation of an emotionless human being. After surgery to remove a brain tumor, Elliot was described by one of his doctors as having no emotion: "I never saw a tinge of emotion in my many hours of conversation with him, no sadness, no frustration, no impatience" (Damasio, 1994, 34). Without the capacity to feel, Elliot "lost not only an important part of life's experience but also (the) ability to make decisions. Everything began to seem equally important (or unimportant); all outcomes were equally valued" (Funder, 2004, 224). To identify with Elliot and appreciate the role of emotions in decision-making, consider the commonplace restaurant experience of having difficulty deciding what to eat. After reading the menu several times, you find yourself immobilized, unable to place an order with your server. The problem is not a lack of information; the problem is that nothing on the menu elicits a feeling. (A dining preference often is expressed in terms of a feeling, e.g. "I feel like having a steak.)

While the "Terminator's" ability to stay on task is something to be envied, Elliot's indecisiveness is not. Further, although the "Terminator" has a remarkable human-like appearance, it lacks the capacity to question its programming. It has no free will; therefore, it is not responsible for its behavior. Philosopher Thomas Ellis Katen posits that free will and its concomitant responsibility substantially define a human being:

> Human beings come to terms with life and understand themselves as human through such experiences as re-

> gret, remorse, sorrow, and guilt. This entire mode of functioning cannot be simply discounted. Free will is a working assumption of human existence as it has evolved throughout history, and moral experience is an all-important aspect of that history (1973, 318).

Regret, remorse, sorrow, and guilt are not pleasant emotions and life without these unpleasantries is attractive. However, an emotionless life would also preclude the experiences of contentment, happiness, love, and exuberance. Concerning exuberance, Kay Redfield Jamison has written:

> Exuberance is an abounding, ebullient, effervescent emotion. It is kinetic and unrestrained, joyful, irrepressible. It is not happiness, although they share a border. It is instead, at its core, a more restless billowing state. Certainly, it is no lulling sense of contentment: exuberance leaps, bubbles, and overflows, propels its energy through troop and tribe (2004, 4).

Akin to exuberance is enthusiasm, which is derived from the Greek words en and theos, meaning "a god within." Georg Wilhelm Friedrich Hegel taught, "In the world nothing great has ever been accomplished without passion" (2012). Louis Pasteur expressed a similar sentiment when he wrote," The grandeur of human actions is measured by the inspiration from which they spring. Happy is he who bears a god within, and obeys it" (Dubos, 1950, 391).

Emotions are necessary for the connection of human beings to each other. The Capgras syndrome is a fascinating condition that can result from brain injury to the right frontal lobe.

> Apparently what happens to these patients is that they see someone who is near and dear to them, and whose

> form they recognize readily, but then they fail to feel any emotional response to this recognition. Imagine, if you can, seeing your parents, your siblings, or your boyfriend or girlfriend and feeling nothing emotional at all. What would you think? What these patients conclude, it seems, is that these cannot possibly be the people they appear to be, and that the only possible interpretation (one conjured up by the uninjured left frontal lobe) is that they must have been replaced by nearly identical doubles (Funder, 2004, 223).

The science fiction movie, "I, Robot," referred to in chapter one, includes that heartbreaking scene in which a robot saves the life of a policeman at the expense of a little girl's. (As a reminder or if the first chapter has not been read, "I Robot" is set in the year 2035 when robots have been developed to do the unskilled work formerly done by human beings.) The scene is an automobile accident in which two cars are forced off a bridge and into the water below. A robot dives into the water and rescues the policeman who unsuccessfully tries to redirect the robot to the other car, sinking fast with the child in it. The robot, acting solely on logic, tells the officer the girl's survival probability is eleven percent and his is forty-five percent. The robot cannot make a distinction between a child and an adult and cannot appreciate how the policeman will feel about surviving if the girl drowns. It lacks the emotionally driven imperative that adults put the safety of children above their own (2004).

Conclusion

Some might argue that a cost-benefit analysis of emotions is academic since we have no choice but to have feelings. True, an emotionless life is not an option. Still, the question has philosophical and psychological value. "What is a human being?" is one of four questions Immanuel Kant posited as encapsulating the study of philosophy (Katen, 1973, 91). Since emotions are integral to human beings, answering Kant's question requires that attention be given to them. Psychotherapy is engagement with a mental health professional in order to examine, understand, and possibly change one's thoughts, behaviors, and *feelings*. Further, aside from psychotherapy, people are curious about their feelings, ranging from joy to despair and all emotional points in-between.

If the benefits and burdens of emotions could be placed on a balance scale, the cost-effectiveness of emotions could be determined easily and empirically. But their positive and negative aspects cannot be quantified, making an objective assessment impossible. This being the case, one means for addressing this issue is to extrapolate a conclusion from three facts.

1. Owing to creation or evolution, we have feelings. Therefore, either by design or adaptation, it has been determined that human beings are better off with emotions than without them. Further, an evolutionist might argue that were it not for emotions the human race could not have survived. Certainly, Vincent van Gogh was unfamiliar with the theory of evolution, but his reflection on emotions, quoted at the beginning of this chapter, would be agreeable to an evolutionist: "But are not this struggle and even the mistakes one may make better, and do they not develop us more, than if we kept systematically away from emotions?" (2012).

2. Life is enriched by positive emotions that would not exist but for negative emotions. The feeling of contentment from having acted courageously is made

possible by the recognition of danger and emotion of fear. The exhilaration from the acceptance of a declaration of love is preceded by the anxiety that accompanies the possibility of rejection. Before the exuberance of winning an Olympic gold medal was the potential for profound disappointment. (Jim McKay, the host of ABC's "Wide World of Sports," reminded us every week that athletic competition includes "the thrill of victory and the agony of defeat.")

3. Some decisions, if they are to be justified, require emotion as a part of the decision-making process. The robot in "I, Robot" lacked the capacity to feel. Being human, it's unlikely you believe rescuing the policeman was the right decision . (This is not to say that emotions should be a part of all decisions-making.)

As a psychotherapist with twenty-five years of clinical experience, I report that some patients and moments are indelibly memorable. One such moment occurred with a Vietnam veteran who reflected on his combat experience and said, "Vietnam, Vietnam, I wouldn't trade the experience for a million dollars; I wouldn't give a dime to do it over." He went on to say that during his thirteen months there he never felt more alive or more important or more connected to others. He added that he never felt more afraid. Kay Redfield Jamison has written similarly of the bipolar disorder that has plagued, yet strangely, enriched her life:

> I have often asked myself whether, given the choice, I would choose to have manic-depressive illness. If lithium were not available to me, or didn't work for me, the answer would be a simple no – and it would be an answer laced with terror. But lithium does work for me, and therefore I suppose I can afford to pose the

> question. Strangely enough I think I would choose to have it. Depression is awful beyond words or sounds or images; I would not go through an extended one again. ...
>
> So why would I want anything to do with this illness? Because I honestly believe that as a result of it I have felt more things, more deeply; had more experiences, more intensely; loved more, and been more loved; laughed more often for having cried more often; appreciated more the springs, for all the winters; worn death "as close as dungarees," appreciated it – and life – more ... (1995, 217-218).

Obviously, if we never had emotions we could neither miss nor conceptualize them. But we do have them and few among us would sign up unreservedly for *affective neutralization* surgery. Fear is discomforting but contributes to safety and survival. Implicit in the intoxicating experience of love is the pain associated with abandonment, disappointment and rejection. An adage that well describes this pain is, "You don't die from a broken heart, you just wish you did." Notwithstanding, the Tin Woodsman didn't return his heart to the Wizard of Oz when it was broken.

The virtues of knowledge and wisdom have their downside: "For with much wisdom comes much sorrow; the more knowledge, the more grief" (Ecclesiastes 1:18, *New International Version*). The same is true of desirable emotions. Thomas Gray's oft quoted, "Ignorance is bliss" communicates that one route to the desirable feeling of bliss is the undesirable state of ignorance (1742, 99-100). Intuition and life experience forcefully argue that emotions are more a blessing than a curse, more a benefit than an unredeeming burden.

Operational Questions: How We Feel and Behave

8. When Is Our Behavior Abnormal?

One of the unpardonable sins, in the eyes of most people, is for a man to go about unlabeled. The world regards such a person as the police do an unmuzzled dog, not under proper control.

- T.H. Huxley

To some extent, sanity is a matter of conformity.

- John Nash

During football practice in the fall of 2008, Mesa State College football player Trevor Wikre injured the pinkie finger of his right hand. When told by doctors that the injury, a compound fracture, might not ever heal completely, Wikre said, "Then cut it off," explaining that it was his senior year and he did not want to miss his last football season (Ballard, 2008).With understandable reluctance, the doctor amputated the finger just below the knuckle joint and Wikre went on to play his final year. Is this an example of abnormal behavior? If so, then what about a man who not only chose to have his arm amputated, but removed the limb himself?

The man, Aron Ralston, was trapped in a cave when an 800 pound boulder shifted and pinned his right arm against the cave's wall. After five days of futility he decided to do the only thing that would save his life. Neither his self-surgery nor his description of it in his book, *Between a Rock and a Hard Place*, is delicate. In it he describes the three step procedure of cutting (flesh, muscle, and tendons), breaking (ulna and radius bones), and snipping (nerve). Weakened by a forty-five pound weight loss, Ralston nevertheless accomplished the self-amputation that saved his life (Malikow, 2007, 77-78).

Two self-determined amputations, one in order to play a football season; the other to save a life. Although both decisions arose from abnormal circumstances, is either of them "sick" in the sense of an indication of mental illness? This question is not posed as part of addressing the morality of these decisions but to consider *what constitutes abnormal behavior* and *which abnormal behaviors qualify as a mental illness*. Implicit in this deliberation is the question: *Who determines what is (and is not) sick behavior?*

When Supreme Court Justice Potter Stewart admitted to his inability to construct a legal definition for pornography he added, "but I know it when I see it" (Jacobellis v. Ohio, 1964). There are those who would say the same concerning *abnormal* behavior. Even if it is impossible to define it precisely, it is often easily recognizable. As is often the case with oversimplifications, there is a kernel of truth in Justice Stewart's assertion. However, mental health professionals could not effectively function if his characterization of pornography were to be applied to *psychopathology* (the study of mental illness) and used as a guide for diagnosis. Like beauty, abnormal behavior is often in the eye of the beholder. Accordingly, the American Psychiatric Association's *Diagnostic and Statistical Manual* (fourth edition, published in 1994) contains 410 psychiatric illnesses. (The first edition, published in 1952, had 60 mental illnesses. A fifth edition is due for publication in May 2013, after the completion of this book.)

The renown (some would say notorious) psychiatrist Thomas Szasz has posited that the DSM-IV has 410 too many mental illnesses. Over thirty years ago, in *The Myth of Mental Illness*, he wrote:

> It is widely believed that mental illness is a type of disease, and that psychiatry is a branch of medicine; and yet, whereas people readily think of and call themselves "sick," they rarely think of and call themselves "mentally sick." The reason for this ... is really quite simple: a person might feel sad or elated; insignificant or grandiose; suicidal or homicidal, and so forth; he is, however, not likely to recognize himself as mentally ill or insane; that he is, is more likely to be suggested by someone else. This, then, is why bodily diseases are characteristically treated with the consent of the patient, while mental diseases are characteristically treated without his consent. (Individuals who nowadays seek private psychoanalytic or psychotherapeutic help do not, as a rule, consider themselves either "sick" or "mentally sick," but rather view their difficulties as problems in living and the help they receive as a type of counseling.) In short, psychiatric diagnoses are stigmatizing labels (1974, pp. xi-xii).

Dr. Szasz offers a minority report from the psychiatric community, he raises a valid question: *On what objective, scientific basis do mental health professionals determine that a behavior is abnormal and to be considered a diagnosable mental illness?* He concedes that it is reasonable to speak of physical illnesses since there are standards for various organs and systems of the human body. For example, hearts and kidneys can be described as functioning at fifty-percent efficiency since heart and kidney functioning can be quantified. Szasz reasons that since mental illnesses are determined according to behavior and no standard for behavior exists, then the concept of mental illness is mythical. Psychiatrist and author Irvin Yalom has made a similar, although less provocative observation of diagnosis:

> Though diagnosis is unquestionably critical in treatment considerations for many severe conditions with a biological substrate (for example, schizophrenia, bipolar disorders, major affective disorders, temporal lobe epilepsy, drug toxicity, organic or brain diseases from toxins, degenerative causes, or infectious agents), diagnosis is often *counterproductive* in the everyday psychotherapy of less severely impaired patients. ... A colleague of mine brings this point home to his psychiatric residents by asking, "If you are in personal psychotherapy or are considering it, what DSM-IV diagnosis do you think your therapist could justifiably use to describe someone as complicated as you?" (2002, pp. 4-5)

In this vein, it should be pointed out that among mental health professionals there is no definition of *abnormal behavior*. This is not to say that psychiatrists and psychologists are on their own to determine which behaviors are abnormal. First, they are not at liberty to go beyond the *DSM-IV* when diagnosing. (More will be said about the *DSM-IV* later in this chapter.) Second, in the absence of a definition for *abnormal behavior*, mental health professionals discuss abnormality in terms of three manifestations: *statistical, dysfunctional*, and *distressful*.

Epidemiology is the study of the statistical occurrence of a disease or condition. To say that one-percent of Americans have schizophrenia or annually there are 40,000 suicides committed in the United States is to make an epidemiological statement. When assessing an individual for diagnosis, a question that is considered is: "Is this person acting differently from most people?" This question cannot always be answered since statistics are not available for every behavior. Further, perhaps less than fifty-percent of people play golf, but this cannot be statistically verified and, even if it could, it certainly would not establish playing golf as a mental illness. Another assessment question is, "Does this behavior prevent this person from meeting responsibilities?" For example, the alcoholic who chronically misses work and continually fails to pay bills because of excessive drinking is dysfunctional. A third appraisal question is, "Is this behavior upsetting to the person engaged in it?" An illustration would be those agoraphobics (abnormal fear of open spaces) who are frustrated by their inability to venture outside their homes. When a behavior meets all three criteria for abnormality, it is likely to be found in the *DSM-IV*.

The word diagnosis derives from a Greek word (*diagignoskein*) meaning "to perceive apart from other things." The work of diagnosis in mental health, as in medicine, must be done with great care. Since diagnosis implies treatment, to misdiagnose makes mistreatment probable. Further, a mental health diagnosis often carries with it a stigma. In addition, such a diagnosis might place an individual at a disadvantage when applying for a job or pursuing custody of children in a divorce. Once labeled, a person is perceived differently. This was demonstrated in a well-known study conducted by Stanford University psychologist David Rosenhan.

In a 1973 investigation immortalized as the "Sane in an Insane Place" experiment, Rosenhan and seven of his colleagues were able to get admitted to a psychiatric hospital after presenting themselves by faking a symptom associated with schizophrenia (auditory hallucinations). All eight were appropriately diagnosed according to this symptom and remained in the hospital for an average of nineteen days. After admission, the eight "patients" ceased complaining that they were "hearing voices" and returned to their normal behavior. In addition, they provided honest life histories in their therapy. (These histories were normal and not suggestive of schizophrenia.) What is remarkable is that the clinicians from whom Rosenhan and his confederates received treatment never revised the original diagnosis. In fact, the normal behavior and life histories of the "patients" were interpreted by the professionals as schizophrenic. Strange is that the professionals did not recognize the difference between the "patients" who stopped feigning schizophrenia and the ward's actual schizophrenic patients who were showing symptoms (Rosenhan, 1973).

Another instance illustrating the elusive nature of diagnosis is the *alien abductee* research of the late John Mack. A psychiatrist, Pulitzer Prize recipient in literature, and a Harvard University professor, Dr. Mack lost the esteem of some of his colleagues when he developed an interest in the experiences reported by people who claimed to have been taken up by alien beings, subjected to physical examinations, and then returned to earth. Pressured by others of his profession to dismiss the *abductees* as psychotic (withdrawn from reality), he steadfastly refused. Mack maintained that while he could not affirm the claim of the *abductees*, neither could he diagnose them as psychotic. (They seemed quite normal to him except for their claim of abduction, which they admitted seemed incredible.) He explained his refusal to make such a diagnosis by saying that while he could not confirm their claim of abduction, he did not feel compelled to label them psychotic. He refused to diagnose by the process of elimination and suggested that they might have had an experience for which there is no existing category. In a BBC interview he said:

> I would never say, yes, there were aliens taking people. (But) I would say there is a compelling, powerful phenomenon here that I can't account for in any other way – that's mysterious. Yet I can't know what it is but it seems to me that it invites a deeper, further inquiry (Mack, 2009).

Cultural mores also enter into a consideration of abnormal behavior. It is plausible to say that intentionally burning one's self to death is the act of a profoundly mentally ill person. Yet, there are at least two cultures in which immolation was not only acceptable, but honorable. One such instance was the Hindu funeral ritual of *suttee* in which a devoted wife would place herself in the flames cremating her husband's body. (This practice was outlawed in India in 1948 when it was under British rule.) Another instance of a culturally acceptable immolation was the practice of some Buddhist monks in the 1960s and 70s who protested the Vietnam War by burning themselves to death.

A well-publicized case of a collision of cultures occurred in 1995 in Dallas, Texas when an Albanian man, Sadri Krasniqi, was charged with the molestation his four year-old daughter, Lima. Eventually, Mr. Krasniqi was acquitted when the court was convinced that although touching a daughter's private parts is fondling in this country, such behavior is acceptable in his homeland of Kosovo, Serbia. (It should be noted that sexual activity with a child is unthinkable among Albanians, but touching is not considered sexual contact.) Mr. Krasniqi's behavior with his daughter constitutes child molestation by this country's legal statutes and is considered pedophilia by the American Psychiatric Association's standards.

At this point, a reasonable question is: What is normal behavior? Alternatively stated, what is mental health? The noted author and psychiatrist M. Scott Peck offered the following definition: "Mental health is a commitment to reality at all costs" (1978, 44). Of course, who has the final word on *reality*? The oft quoted maxim, *perception is reality*, implies that reality is subjectively experienced and, therefore, individually defined. If all claims to reality are equally valid, then approximately forty years ago there were three simultaneous visitations of Jesus Christ to a Michigan psychiatric hospital. In *The Three Christs of Ypsilanti* psychologist Milton Rokeach describes his therapy with three delusional men, all of whom claimed to be Jesus Christ (Rokeach, 1964). Dr. Rokeach seized this unusual opportunity to see if he could use group therapy with the three men to dispel their shared delusion. He was unable to accomplish this treatment goal. Obviously, perception is reality cannot mean that anything and everything a person might believe constitutes reality. If the maxim is to have any utility, it must mean that one way for one person to understand another would be to understand the other person's grasp of reality.

The "bible" for mental health professionals is the *Diagnostic and Statistical Manual*, now in its fourth edition. (As stated previously, the fifth edition is anticipated for 2013.) The *DSM – IV* is a product of the American Psychiatric Association and it provides criteria for the diagnosis of mental health conditions and suggestions for their treatment. In addition, it furnishes mental health professionals with a common vocabulary. The *DSM – IV* format for reports on patients requires evaluations in five different areas, each referred to as an axis. Below is an example of a *DSM – IV* evaluation.

Patient's Name: *John Doe*

Axis I: Clinical Disorder: *depression and substance abuse (alcohol)*

Axis II: Personality Disorder: *antisocial personality disorder*

Axis III: General Medical Conditions: *diabetes, hypertension, and obesity*

Axis IV: Psychosocial and Environmental Problems: *unemployed and marital separation*

Axis V: Global Assessment of Functioning:* 65

**The patient's functioning is assessed on a scale of 1 to 100 with 1 being very low. This assessment evaluates the patient in three areas: social relations with family and friends, occupational functioning, and use of leisure time.*

Although the *DSM – IV* provides mental health professionals with a shared vocabulary, psychological misnomers and misunderstandings abound in common discourse. It can be surprising to those outside of the profession to learn of the terms that are either not in the *DSM – IV* or not used by professionals in the way those terms are understood by laypersons. Many who disagree with Dr. Szasz's view of *mental illness* still take exception to the use of the term *nervous breakdown* or the suggestion that insane is a psychological term. What is commonly referred to as a nervous breakdown (a state of complete or almost complete dysfunctionality) is technically a *decompensation.* (Actually, nervous breakdown more accurately describes spinal cord injured patients because paraplegics and quadriplegics have a disruption of the central nervous system.)

Similarly, *insane* is not a psychological term but a legal category. In 1843 Daniel McNaughton, in an attempt to assassinate British Prime Minister Robert Peel, mistakenly killed Peel's secretary, Edmund Drummond. At McNaughton's trial the legal concept of *insanity* was introduced when nine witnesses who knew him described his typical behavior in a way that a contemporary psychiatrist would consider paranoid schizophrenia. To the consternation of Queen Victoria, the court ruled that the defendant was incapable of understanding his killing of Drummond as a morally wrong, illegal act. In the next decade, courts in the United States adopted the McNaughton Rule as the standard for legal insanity: insane individuals are either incapable of understanding certain of their behaviors as illegal or they cannot restrain themselves from these behaviors. In jurisprudence, insanity is the shorthand term for the inability to distinguish right from wrong behavior or the inability to keep one's self from wrong behavior.

Neither is the word *crazy* is a formal, psychological term. Rather, it is a colloquialism suggestive of madness but too imprecise to be of any diagnostic value to a mental health professional. The same is true of the more earthy adjectives *nuts, looney, bananas*, and *fruitcake*.

In addition to misnomers, there are misunderstandings of terms that are part of psychological jargon. *Schizophrenia* is frequently misunderstood as the condition of having multiple personalities. Actually, schizophrenia is a subcategory of *psychosis* (departure from reality), characterized by disordered thinking and speaking often accompanied by *auditory hallucinations* (hearing voices) and *paranoia* (delusions of persecution). Hence, the following poem is psychologically incorrect:

Roses are red,
violets are blue,
I'm a schizophrenic,
and so am I.

In fact, *multiple personality disorder* itself is no longer a formal psychological term, having been supplanted by *dissociative identity disorder*. Similarly, the term *psychopath* has been replaced with antisocial personality disorder as the diagnosis for those who show a chronic indifference and insensitivity to the rights and feelings of others. These changes reflect the periodic updating of the *Diagnostic and Statistical Manual.*

Two terms erroneously used interchangeably are psychotherapy and *counseling*. Technically, they are not synonyms. Psychotherapy is provided to individuals who have been diagnosed with a mental illness as categorized by the *DSM – IV*. These individuals are properly referred to as *patients*. (The word therapy derives from the Greek word *therapeuo* which means "to heal.") In contrast, counseling refers to work conducted with people who are seeking help in addressing certain life issues. For instance, a couple in marriage counseling is not pursuing healing from a mental illness. Hence they are referred to as *clients*, not *patients*.

In spite of the difficulty of distinguishing abnormal from normal behavior, it is a distinction made by mental health specialists nearly every day of their professional lives with varying degrees of consequences for those diagnosed. Psychiatrist Irvin Yalom offers a word of caution concerning the application of the *DSM-IV* categories:

> Remember that clinicians involved in formulating previous, now discarded, diagnostic systems were competent, proud, and just as confident as the current members of the *DSM-IV* committees. Undoubtedly the time will come when the *DSM-IV* Chinese restaurant menu format will appear ludicrous to mental health professionals (p. 5).

9. What Is Heroism and Why Do We Admire Heroes?

Be not afraid of greatness: some are born great, some achieve greatness, and some have greatness thrust upon them.

- William Shakespeare

I have seen the moment of my greatness flicker, And I have seen the eternal Footman hold my coat, and snicker, And, in short, I was afraid.

- "The Love Song of J. Alfred Prufrock," T.S. Eliot

Heroes are not born, they are cornered.

- Anonymous

In *Everyday Morality*, philosophy professor Mike W. Martin describes this terrifying episode.

> In a wilderness area in a city where I live, a woman was hiking with her five-year-old daughter in 1986. A mountain lion attacked the girl and dragged her into some bushes. The mother's frantic screams were heard by Gregory Ysais, a thirty-six-year-old electronics technician who happened to be hiking in the same area. Without any hesitation Ysais ran to the scene to find the cougar gripping the bloody and squirming child by the back of her neck. Ysais grabbed a branch and repeatedly swung it over the cougar's head. The full-grown cougar responded with threatening roars and quick strikes with his huge paws. After a few

> minutes the cougar dropped the child long enough for her to be pulled away.
>
> Ysais later reported that he had never been in a life-and-death situation before and had never thought of himself as a hero: "I didn't give it much thought. I just heard people crying for help, and I just ran as fast as I could. I was just doing what I had to do. I couldn't think of anything else" (1986, 121).

Prior to his courageous intervention, Gregory Ysais never thought of himself as a hero. Perhaps he did afterward. Certain is that most people would view his action as heroic even if he did not recognize the danger to himself, calculate the risk, and consider the option of avoidance.

An answer to the question, "Who is a hero?" requires that several other questions first be addressed: How is hero defined? What are the characteristics that distinguish a hero from a non-hero? Does a single heroic act make a person a hero? Are people heroes if they acted in the line of duty or in response to a calling? Does heroism require the elements of choice and/or overcoming fear? Is it possible to be heroic living an ordinary, unrecognized life?

How is hero defined?

The *American Heritage Dictionary*, (pp. 617-618) offers six definitions of hero. Two of these definitions will not be a part of this treatise: (1) "a sandwich of heroic size made with a small loaf of crusty bread split lengthwise, containing lettuce, condiments, and a variety of meats and cheeses" and, (2) "any male regarded as a potential lover or protector." (My apologies to Subway and Olive Oyl's Popeye.) The four definitions that remain are relevant to the matter at hand; they refer to mythology, courage, fiction, and accomplishment.

In mythology and legend a hero is a being, often born of one mortal and one divine parent, who is favored by the gods, endowed with great courage and strength, and celebrated for bold exploits. Achilles embodies this definition. In *The Iliad*, he ponders the glory that will be his if he remains in Troy and fights in the Trojan War. This glory, however, will be at the expense of his life. (The Greek word for "glory" is *kleos*, the fame which is often heard through a song or poem.)

> My mother Thetis tells me there are two ways in which I may meet my end. If I stay here and fight then I shall lose my safe homecoming but I will have glory that is unwilting. Whereas if I go home my glory will die, but it will be a long time before the outcome of death shall take me (Homer, 1998, 9.410-416).

Perhaps the most common understanding of a hero is one who is noted for feats of courage or nobility of purpose; especially someone who has risked or sacrificed his life. The aforementioned Gregory Ysais fits this description as does the unnamed pilot in Kay Jamison's memoir, *An Unquiet Mind*. Faced with the dilemma of parachuting from his malfunctioning jet to safety or staying with the plane and guiding it away from a schoolyard full of children, he chose the latter and died in a fiery crash. Years later, Jamison, one of those children, wrote of him: "The dead pilot became a hero, transformed into a scorchingly vivid, completely impossible ideal for what was meant by the concept of duty" (1995, 13).

A familiar use of the word hero is "the principle character in a novel, poem, or dramatic presentation" (*American Heritage Dictionary*, 617). *Les Miserables'* Jean Valjean is one of countless literary and theatrical protagonists who fits this characterization (Hugo, 1987).

Individuals of noteworthy achievement often are referred to as heroes. Baseball legend Babe Ruth, Civil War general Robert E. Lee, and civil rights activist Martin Luther King, Jr. are men of accomplishment who enjoy heroic status.

What are the characteristics of a hero?

How is a hero distinguished from a non-hero? In situations that call for heroic action, are there only two possibilities for those in a position to respond? Returning to Gregory Ysais, was he in a situation in which he was going to be either a hero or coward? He acted heroically, but would he have been a coward had he not intervened? Were there only two options available to him: either engage in a struggle with the mountain lion or allow the animal to have its way with the child without interference? Had he stood by and watched, the outcome for the girl would have been the same as if he had walked away from the horrific scene. Further, if he had not intervened, would he be a villain, even though he was not the one bringing harm to the child?

In addition, since Ysais was not seeking an opportunity to act heroically, it is accurate to say that he had greatness thrust upon him. He came upon a crisis and reacted in an exemplary manner. (Interesting is that the Mandarin Chinese characters that combine to be translated to crisis in English are "danger" and "opportunity.") Certainly, anyone who orchestrated a situation for the purpose of acquiring heroic status would not be a hero. An episode of a television program of many years ago, "Hill Street Blues," featured a police officer who had accidentally shot and killed a little boy. Guilt-ridden and disgraced, he seemed to have made a start at restoring his soiled reputation when he rescued a child from a house fire. When it was discovered that he had arranged for the fire to create an opportunity for heroism his ignominy became even greater.

Does a single act of heroism make a person a hero?

One of the ways in which we can know ourselves is to consider that we are who we are most of the time (Malikow, 2010, 106-108). Heroic is but one of 17,953 personality traits (Allport, 1936). Heroic differs from traits that can be demonstrated daily like patience, self-discipline, and generosity. Occasions to act heroically are few, and many people never encounter even one opportunity for a flickering moment of greatness, let alone fifteen minutes of fame.

One way to consider the sufficiency of a single courageous act to establish someone as a hero is to decide if an opportunity generates heroism or elicits it. In *The Wizard of Oz*, the Cowardly Lion entering the witch's castle to rescue Dorothy did not create courage in the faltering lion (Baum, 2000). Rather, Dorothy's abduction provided the opportunity for the lion's dormant courage to be activated. The lyrics from the song "Tin Man" include an analysis that also applies to the lion: "Oz never did nothing to the tin man, that he didn't already have" (Bunnell, 2000). This assessment suggests there are people who never encounter a situation that would awaken their latent courage, implying there are many unrealized heroes among us.

This is not to say that courage cannot be developed. What is courage if not the subordination of fear to duty and accomplishing the more difficult thing? Courage requires self-discipline, a trait that can be nurtured. The noted biologist Thomas Huxley was so convinced of this he wrote: "The chief purpose of education is to train a person to do what he ought to do, when it ought to be done, whether he feels like it or not" (Wheelock, 1910, 33). If the potential for heroism resides in any of us, it is because of internalized values that enable us to recognize those things that have greater worth than our comfort, safety and, in rare circumstances, self-preservation. Courage is well described in the movie, "The Princess Diaries:"

> Courage is not the absence of fear but rather the judgment that something else is more important than fear. The brave may not live forever but the cautious do not live at all. From now on you are traveling the road between who you think you are and who you can be. (Cabot, 2008).

Heroes are those whose well-developed self-discipline and discernment enable them to rise to the occasions that call for courage. Courage is not created by those occasions, rather, it is a by-product of the self-discipline, values, and moral code that have developed over time.

"Assume the virtue, if you have it not," wrote Shakespeare (Hamlet, 3.4.151). There are virtues that can be feigned, but courage is not one of them. Brave and noble deeds are empirical demonstrations of courage; without courage there would be no courageous acts. For this reason, a single, heroic act is sufficient to qualify an individual as a hero.

However, it is reasonable to ask if subsequent failures of courage call for an individual's reclassification as a coward. An inspirational song asks for, "one moment in time when I'm more than I thought I could be" (Hammond and Bettis, 1988). As previously stated, we are who we are most of the time. Notwithstanding, it is also true that we are who we are in our best moments. These characterizations are not contradictory. No single maxim can capture the essence of any human being, many are needed. Each one provides a perspective. If only once we have exceeded our self-perceived capability, we have been that person, even if for just one moment in time. A new standard of excellence has been established and with it higher expectations, as well as an increased probability for disappointment.

Are people heroes if they acted in the line of duty or in response to a calling?

On January 15, 2009 U.S. Airways pilot Chesney "Sully" Sullenberger landed airliner flight 1549 on the Hudson River after a flock of birds collided with the plane, disabling both engines. One-hundred and fifty-five passengers were grateful for this unconventional landing. It would seem odd to question Captain Sullenberger's status as a national hero on the ground that safely landing airplanes is part of his job description. Similarly, it would seem odd, actually ludicrous, to question if firefighters who entered the World Trade Center towers on September 11, 2001 are heroes since entering burning buildings is what they were supposed to do.

"People keep telling me it was a heroic thing to do. In my opinion it was just the right thing to do" (Hartsock, 05/10/10). These are the words of Dave Hartsock, a skydiving instructor who was strapped to his student, Shirley Dygert, in what is called a tandem jump. (Tandem jumps are used in a first jump experience.) When their first parachute opened partially and the reserve chute became entangled in the first one, instructor and student went into a death spiral at 10,000 feet. At 500 feet and descending at 40 miles per hour, Hartsock skillfully managed the control toggles and rotated his position under Dygert so that his body would act as a cushion and break her fall. He is now a quadriplegic with only slight movement in his right arm. Hartsock does not think of himself as a hero. "I was the one who was completely responsible for her safety. What other choices were there?" (Hartsock).

In 1956, Christian missionary Jim Eliot and four of his fellow evangelists were slain by Waudani tribesman in Ecuador. The five men were speared to death by the very people to whom they believe they had been called to present the gospel of Jesus Christ. By virtue of their ultimate sacrifice, these missionaries are martyrs, heroes of the Christian faith. Nobel laureate and humanitarian Mother Teresa of Calcutta also carried on her work in response to a calling, thereby sacrificing whatever other life she might have had. Sainthood, which is her inevitable status, is another expression of religious heroism. These missionaries and Mother Teresa did their work neither as a job nor a profession, but in obedience to a calling. However admirable such obedience might be, can it be considered heroic if it is in response to a divine directive?

Merely doing one's job or carrying out a divinely inspired mission is heroic when the accomplishment is extraordinary or the sacrifice is great. Captain Sullenberger was trained and hired to land airplanes on runways - not rivers. The firefighters who entered the towers of the World Trade Center were trained for extinguishing fires and making rescues in a variety of situations, but not the one that confronted them on 9/11. (As far as we know, none of them refused to go into the towers saying, "Since I am not trained for this, this is not part of my job.")

Does heroism require the elements of choice and/or overcoming fear?

Aristotle's Principle of the Golden Mean characterizes a virtue as the apex between two extremes, both of which are vices. From this construction, the virtue of courage is the zenith between the vices of recklessness and cowardice. Recklessness is expressed by action without an appreciation for danger. Without the recognition of danger, there can be no experience of fear. Inaction resulting from the awareness of danger is cowardice. The Aristotilian concept of courage requires action despite fear. The application of the Principle of the Golden Mean to courage gives rise to two questions: Is an action heroic if it did not require overcoming fear? And, is an action heroic if there was no choice but to act? Gregory Ysais said he intervened without thinking, making his action more a reflex than a behavior. If he acted without considering the danger and the option of non-involvement, then his reaction does not conform to Aristotle's formula for courage. Similarly, it could be argued that Islamic jihadist suicide bombers and World War II Japanese kamikaze pilots cannot be heroes since their cultural conditioning precluded authentic choice-making.

Further, it is not always clear as to whether or not someone actually has a choice. Did Aron Ralston, the trapped mountain climber who amputated his arm rather than die in a cave, really have a choice? His options were to remain pinned until he died an agonizing death from starvation or experience the ineffable pain of removing his arm with a small knife. (Is it any wonder that the title of his memoir is *Between a Rock and a Hard Place*?)

Individuals who subordinated fear or endured pain to achieve something perceived of greater value have acted commendably, if not heroically. This being said, people also can act heroically without confronting fear or the possibility of avoidance. Reconsider Ysais and Ralston and ask, "Could I have done that?" If your answer is, "I don't think so," or "I don't know, but I would hope so," or "No, but I admire what they did," then this is sufficient to establish them as heroic. Of course, this is a sentimentalist argument. (Sentimentalism is the belief that some knowledge cannot be acquired from reason or scientific demonstration, but only from the feeling that something is true.) The counter to this would be a logical argument, perhaps in the form of a syllogism:

<u>Major Premise</u>

All heroic acts include the subordination of fear and/or option of avoidance.

Minor Premise

Ysais fighting off a mountain lion included neither subordination of fear nor the option of avoidance.

Conclusion

Therefore, Ysais did not engage in an act of heroism.

The flaw in this syllogism resides in the major premise. While it may be true that all subordination of fear is a demonstration of heroism, it does not follow that all acts of heroism include the subordination of fear. (The same can be said about the option of avoidance.)

Stanford University psychologist Philip Zombardo, founder of the Heroic Imagination Project, believes that just as a sociopath is the product of nurturing, so also a hero can be developed:

> We have been saddled too long with (a) mystical view of heroism. We assume heroes are demigods. But they're not. A hero is just an ordinary person who does something extraordinary. I believe we can use science to teach people how to do that (Lehrer, 2010).

Is it possible to be a hero living an ordinary, unrecognized life?

It is not customary to buttress a philosophical position by citing a professional athlete. However, an observation made by basketball superstar Charles Barkley is relevant to the question of whether an ordinary, unpublicized person can be a hero. In the wake of the revelation of National Football League quarterback Michael Vick's dog-fighting fiasco, Barkley challenged the assumption that athletes are role models: "Just because I dunk a basketball doesn't mean I should raise your kids" (12/25/10). He vehemently denies that he, Michael Vick, Michael Jordan or any other sports celebrity is a hero or role model for children. Barkley posits that each father bears that responsibility for his own children. Zimbardo agrees with Barkley: "One of the problems with our culture is that we've replaced heroes with celebrities. We worship people who haven't done anything" (Lehrer, 2010).

For some, a philosophical position articulated by Charles Barkley does not carry sufficient weight to be convincing. (Anyone who has seen Barkley would recognize him as a man who carries considerable weight.) Such an objection, however, would be an *ad hominem* argument. Heroism is expressed moment-by-moment all over the world when extraordinary, unpublicized acts of virtue occur. This opinion does not devalue heroism, rather it elevates it to something each of us can do, perhaps even frequently.

10. Are We Capable of Meaningful Change?

Quando una persona fu nato rotonda, non puoi morire quadrata. (When a person is born round, he doesn't die square.)

- Italian Proverb

... if anyone is in Christ, he is a new creation; the old has gone, the new has come!

- 2 Corinthians 5:17 (New International Version)

In contrast to lawyers, psychiatrists have to tolerate very few jokes about their profession. One of the few is this combination "light bulb/psychiatrist" joke:

> Question: How many psychiatrists does it take to change a light bulb?
>
> Answer: Only one, but the light bulb has to really want to change.

Unlike light bulbs, human beings often have the desire to change and actually can change themselves. *Or can they*? According to the Italian proverb cited above, people cannot change. The excerpt from Paul's letter to the Corinthians, also cited above, posits that change is possible owing to a spiritual experience. Among living things, human beings are unique in that they often desire to make a significant change in themselves. If the Italian proverb is correct, then anyone engaged in such an effort is on a fool's errand.

Change Defined and Delineated

The possibility of physical change is not the topic of this chapter. That people can change their bodies through diet and exercise, as well as cosmetic surgery is indisputable. The American Society for Aesthetic Plastic Surgery reported 9.2 million cosmetic surgical and nonsurgical procedures accomplished in 2011 (2012). The topic of this chapter is the possibility of substantial changes in personality.

Synonyms for *change* include *alter, vary, modify, transform*, and *convert*. Rehabilitate is not usually synonymous with change, but the two words are equivalent in the context of a scene from the movie "The Shawshank Redemption," referred to in chapter six. In the scene, at a parole hearing, a convicted murderer is asked, "Are you rehabilitated?" The convict, Ellis Boyd Redding, a man who has spent most of his adult life in prison, recognizes the question as tantamount to asking, "Have you changed?" His eloquent response satisfies the parole board that he is, indeed, a different man. This kind of change constitutes a substantial change in personality - "an individual's characteristic pattern of thinking, feeling, and acting" (Myers, 2011, 553). In a given situation, people are capable of choosing to think optimistically or act kindly or use meditation to calm themselves. A much greater challenge would be to maintain optimism or kindness or calmness as newly embraced personality traits.

The Difficulty of Change

Psychologist Albert Ellis proposed that people resist trying to change because they believe the myth that things must come easily. This belief produces low frustration tolerance and a fear of failure.

> They say to themselves, "Even though it's desirable for me to change in the long run, it's going to be very hard in the short run, and therefore I'll do it tomorrow, I'll do it tomorrow, I'll do it tomorrow."
>
> The other reason for procrastinating about change is fear of failure. "If I change I must have a guarantee that it will work out, everything will be fine, I will succeed, and people will love me. Since I don't have that guarantee, particularly in a new situation, I'll do it tomorrow or I won't do it at all."
>
> A subheading under the fear of failure is fear of disapproval (Wholey, 1997, 44).

Often, change requires learning and abandoning a previously held belief. This is something the renown psychiatrist Thomas Szasz believes occurs more easily for children than adults:

> Every act of conscious learning requires the willingness to suffer an injury to one's self-esteem. This is why young children, before they are aware of their own self-importance, learn so easily; and why older persons, especially if vain or important, cannot learn at all (1973, 18).

Another hinderance to change is fatigue, which breeds impatience. Tired people are vulnerable to quitting. This is why the legendary football coach Vince Lombardi emphasized the importance of conditioning to his players, telling them, "Fatigue makes cowards of us all" (2012). This is consistent with and related to another philosophy he inculcated in his teams: "We never lose, we just run out of time" (2012).

Sir Winston Churchill characterized the Soviet Union's foreign policy as "a puzzle inside a riddle wrapped in an enigma" (1939). This description also fits the celebrated psychiatrist and author Scott Peck. In his writing he emphasized the necessity and benefits of self-discipline. His seminal work, *The Road Less Traveled*, has been translated into twenty languages and is ranked third among all-time bestselling nonfiction books. Yet, this man who wrote, "Discipline is the basic set of tools we need to solve life's problems," admitted to a lack of restraint in his personal life. In another of his books, he candidly confessed to three deficiencies, none of which he changed:

> I am strongly habituated to alcohol. I eagerly look forward to my gin in quite heavy doses at the end of a day. ... For over forty years now I have used smoking, somewhat like alcohol ... and if I ever kick this fierce addiction it will probably only be at a time when I have ceased to write anymore. ... My sexual infidelity is a glaring example of the unreasonableness of romance. ... I always wished I could have been a different kind of person who did not need such an outlet (1995, 28-30, 42-43).

Dr. Peck's failure and self-disappointment demonstrate the insufficiency of conviction, knowledge, and reputation for effecting change. Widely acclaimed in the 1980s and 90s as the guru of self-discipline, he did not lack an understanding of the importance of temperance. He was aware of the dissonance between his teaching and lifestyle. As well, he was troubled by what many saw as his duplicity. Peck's predicament is accurately captured by the writer James Baldwin's assessment: "Not everything that is faced can be changed. But nothing can be changed until it is faced" (2012).

When People Change

Change is difficult, even when it's recognized as something that would be life-enriching or, moreover, life-saving. Nevertheless, change is possible. To substantiate this claim, each of the five explanations for change offered in this section is supplemented by at least one real-life instantiation of meaningful change.

1. A Matter of Life-and-Death

T.S. Eliot wrote, "One starts an action simply because one must do something" (Wholey, 1997, 6). When professional golfer and alcoholic Laura Baugh was told by an emergency room physician that her next drink would be fatal, she purposed to do something. She had been taken to the hospital with spontaneous bleeding (medical term: thrombocytopenia), caused by an alcohol induced reduction of platelets (the blood component necessary for clotting). Facing imminent death, she entered the Betty Ford Clinic in 1996 and has maintained sobriety to the present. This is more than a mere change in a single behavior. Laura Baugh's sobriety required a radical reordering of her life. Her readjusted priorities have taken her from daily drunkenness to exemplary motherhood.

2. A Profound Life Experience

Over twenty-two centuries ago, the Carthaginian general Hannibal defended his nation against a much larger Roman army. Although it has not been confirmed that he said of his mission, "I will either find a way or make one," his brilliance and determination have been established as historical facts. Determination is firmness of purpose, and few have shown a resolve equal to that of Paul Wittgenstein, the one-armed concert pianist referred to in chapter six. Hannibal and Wittgenstein are impressive as examples of determination, but neither made a dramatic change in personality. In fact, their personalities included the trait of determination and it made their accomplishments possible.

In contrast to them is Dr. Ed Rosenbaum, whose determination became a part of his personality from a life experience. His memoir, *A Taste of My Own Medicine*: *When the Doctor Is the Patient*, recounts the diagnosis and treatment of his laryngeal cancer (1988). Dr. Rosenbaum's fear owing to the uncertainty of outcome combined with his frustration with the medical personnel who diagnosed and treated him resulted in a significant change in his personality. Dr. Rosenbaum's style of relating to people changed and his newfound empathy for the gravely ill made him a compassionate patient advocate and physician-teacher. Said Jim Rosenbaum upon the passing of his father in 2009, "He left a legacy and changed the way physicians practice," (2009).

3. Religious Experience

Harvard psychologist Howard Gardner, renown for his Theory of Multiple Intelligences, has wondered: "What happens when we change our minds? And exactly what does it take for a person to change her mind and begin to act on the basis of this shift?" (2004, 1). He believes, "Our minds are changed either because we ourselves want to change them or because something happens in our mental life that warrants a change" (173).

William James, who taught at Harvard a century before Gardner, considered a religious experience as one of those things that happens in the mental life of many people who change their minds:

> We can make ourselves more faithful to a belief of which we have the rudiments, but we cannot create a belief out of whole cloth when our perception actively

> assures us of the opposite. The better mind proposed to us comes to us in that case in the form of pure negation of the only mind we have, and we cannot will a pure negation (1902, 253).

James maintained that a radical reordering of one's *Weltanschauung* (worldview) can be attributed to "forces outside of the conscious individual" (253). The visitation of three spirits to Ebenezer Scrooge in Charles Dickens' *A Christmas Carol* is a literary depiction of the life-changing religious experience James had in mind. Another fictional illustration is Jean Valjean, the protagonist in Victor Hugo's *Les Miserables*. Real-life instantiations of authentic, life-altering spiritual encounters are Charles Colson and Saint Augustine. The former went from illegal activity as the Special Counsel to President Richard Nixon to the founder of a Christian charitable organization – the Prison Fellowship Ministry. The latter abandoned a life of self-indulgence and an academic career to become one of the most influential scholars in the history of the Christianity.

4. Guilt

Viktor Frankl believed life includes three unavoidable tragedies: pain, death, and guilt. He further believed in the human capacity to redeem each of these tragedies and ultimately derive something good from them. In his classic, *Man's Search for Meaning*, he wrote optimistically of guilt, characterizing it as an "opportunity to change one's self for the better" (1984, 162).

Sigmund Freud also believed in the redemptive possibility of guilt. He posited that the development of a conscience (the superego) makes possible guilt which, in turn, can result in moral self-improvement:

> A great change takes place ... through the establishment of a superego ... it is not until now that we should speak of conscience or sense of guilt. At this point the fear of being found out comes to an end; the distinction moreover, between doing something bad and wishing to do it disappears entirely, since nothing can be hidden from the superego, not even thoughts (1961, 86).

In 1969 a celebrated, hugely successful lawyer named Gerry Spence divorced his wife, Anna, simply because he had fallen in love with another woman. He did this in spite of agonizing guilt over hurting Anna, who had done nothing to displease him and desperately wanted to remain his wife. Even Spence would admit that he did not act honorably by having an affair and disrupting the lives of Anna and their four children. In his biography, he describes a change that took place on the day he married his second wife, Imaging, - a change driven largely by guilt:

> "We gotta make this thing work, Imaging," I said. "If we don't we've screwed ourselves good." "And everybody else," she said. If love meant anything it had to be responsible – we said things like that. I knew the booze was in the way. She knew it, too. It had to go ((1996, 420).

Spence concedes there was nothing meritorious in his divorce, which was motivated by his passion. That passion notwithstanding, he is offered here as an example of a meaningful change driven by guilt.

Boxing legend Muhammed Ali expressed regret over the womanizing of his youth with these words:

> I used to chase women all the time. And I won't say it was right, but look at all the temptations I had. I was young, handsome, heavyweight champion of the world. Women were always offering themselves to me. ... running around, living that kind of life. It hurt my wife, it offended God. It never really made me happy. ... So I did wrong; I'm sorry. And all I'll say as far as running around chasing women is concerned, that's all past. I've got a good wife now, and I'm lucky to have her (Malikow, 2012, 28).

While neither Spence nor Ali deserves commendation for his extramarital activity, both exemplify meaningful change attributable, at least in part, to guilt.

5. Love

In the hit song, "Evil Ways," Carlos Santana admonishes his potential lover: "You've got to change your evil ways, Baby, before I start loving you" (1969). The song doesn't tell if the requested change occurred, but even if it didn't, there are real-life instances of change motivated by love. Laura Baugh, previously used as an example of a "life or death" change, became an exemplary mother. In her memoir, *Out of the Rough*, she attributes her recovery and determination to survive to her love for her seven children (1999).

The existential novelist and playwright Jean-Paul Sartre characterized love as slavery. He believed the desire of a lover is to possess the beloved. If possessed, the beloved is reduced to the status of a human possession, which is a slave. An antithetical analysis of love is found in the New Testament, where love is described as "not self-seeking" (1 Corinthians 13:5, *New International Version*).

Love is a profoundly tender, passionate affection for another person, carrying with it deep concern for the beloved. To love is to be committed to the best interests of the other. In the romantic comedy, "As Good as It Gets," Jack Nicholson's curmudgeonly character tells the woman of his affection, played by Helen Hunt, "You make me want to be a better man" (1997). In this scene there is a confluence of an intrinsic desire for self-change that will be in the best interest of the other.

Conclusion

The eminent psychologist Martin Seligman begins *What You Can Change ... and What You Can't* with this observation:

> Millions are struggling to change: We diet, we jog, we meditate. We adopt new modes of thought to counteract our depressions. We practice relaxation to curb our distress. ... Sometimes it works. But distressingly often, self-improvement and psychotherapy fail. The cost is enormous. We think we are worthless. We feel guilty and ashamed. We believe we have no willpower and that we are failures. We give up trying to change (1993, 3).

Seligman believes many failures at self-improvement result from misguided attempts to change the unchangeable. He agrees with the prayer attributed to Reinhold Niebuhr: "God grant me the serenity to accept the things I cannot change, courage to change the things I can, and wisdom to know the difference." True to the title of his book, Seligman neatly subdivides quests for change into two categories: the possible and the impossible. He does not equate possible with easy. Even the possible requires deliberation, determination, and self-discipline. Also required is planning, since a failure to plan, is a plan to fail.

Deliberation

Change begins with knowing and appreciating why change is desirable. The desire to change can arise as an impulse; sustaining that desire requires careful consideration of why the necessary effort is worthwhile.

Determination

Change cannot be accomplished without self-discipline; without determination there will be no self-discipline. Determination is the conviction that the contemplated change will be life-enriching, if not life-saving.

Self-Discipline

Patience is the ability to endure under difficult circumstances – simply, it is the ability to wait. Self-discipline is the ability to control oneself and one's conduct. Patience and self-discipline, while not synonymous, are interdependent. Shakespeare commended patience as a virtue: "How poor are they that have not patience! What wound did ever heal but by degrees?" (Othello, III, ii). More often than not, change is a process. Without self-discipline and patience, change is unlikely.

Planning

Shakespeare also wrote: "Thou knowest we work by wit, and not by witchcraft; And wit depends on dilatory time" (Othello, III, ii). This is an elegant expression of the idea that accomplishments result from plans, which take time to develop and execute. There is nothing magical about change.

Self-Concept

In addition to deliberation, determination, self-discipline, and planning, there must be a settled belief about one's own life. It is the belief that life is not only worth living, but worth living in an improved state. Albert Camus posited if life is not worth living then suicide is the only logical course. Conversely, he believed if life is worth living then a personally meaningful life should be pursued. Almost certain is that such a life will be punctuated by change.

11. What Is the Place of Sex in the Human Predicament?

Our obsession with our sexuality has led us to develop a wholly false, rather silly, and in the end objectionable view of our natures. Our sexual life is taken to be the measure of our entire life.

- Henry Fairlie

Sex without love is an empty experience, but as empty experiences go it's one of the best.

- Woody Allen

However uncongenial to someone's politics the differences might be, (there) is, in fact, surprising consensus about sex differences.

- Martin Seligman

Sex is something we are (male or female) as well as something we can have. Advertisers are convinced that "sex sells" and educators believe that it deserves its own curriculum (sex education). A popular television series features it ("Sex in the City") and bestselling books analyze it (*Kama Sutra* and *Human Sexual Response*). It's a type of conflict ("the battle of the sexes") and theme of innumerable songs ("Afternoon Delight" and "Do That to Me One More Time"). It's a subcategory of mental illness according to the American Psychiatric Association (psychosexual disorders) and occasionally a long-running news story (Tiger Woods' sex life). Sex is a subject that can be discussed biologically, sociologically, theologically, philosophically, psychologically, or forensically. There is no disputing that sex is a significant part of the human situation and frequent contributor to the human predicament.

The eminent psychologist Martin Seligman has subcategorized sex into five layers, each corresponding to a different aspect of human sexuality (1993):

1. sexual identity: male or female (physical)

2. sexual orientation: homosexual, heterosexual, bisexual, asexual

3. sexual preference: activities that arouse and gratify

4. sexual role: culturally determined occupations and behaviors

5. sexual performance: functionality or dysfunctionality

Imagine being asked to engage in a discussion concerning sex and responding by asking if the conversation will be about *identity, orientation, preference, role*, or *performance.* Seligman's analysis underscores the multivalence of the word sex. To further appreciate the multiple implications of this word, consider each of these layers in juxtaposition to an unusual but actual case or condition associated with it.

Sexual Identity

In 1966 in Winnepeg, Manitoba, the parents of eight month-old Bruce Reimer had him admitted to the hospital for what they believed would be a routine circumcision. Instead of using a scalpel to cut away the foreskin, the doctor opted for cauterization, an unconventional procedure, and accidentally burned off most of the boy's penis. Following the ill-fated circumcision it was determined that Bruce would undergo sexual reassignment surgery. The remnant of his penis was removed and a vagina was surgically constructed for him. In addition, as directed by Dr. John Money, a Johns Hopkins University psychologist, Bruce would be raised as a girl (renamed Brenda) and receive hormonal therapy at puberty. Not understood at the time of the decision to convert Bruce into Brenda was the prenatal neurological development that influences gender.

Years later, after learning of the circumcision, reassignment surgery, and nurturing plan, Reimer finally understood why he always felt like a male trapped in a female body. He committed suicide at age thirty-eight, ending an unhappy life dominated by gender identity confusion. Interviewed shortly before his death, he emphatically asserted, "You can't make a boy into a girl" (Nova, 2001). *Sexual identity* is not as simple a matter as was believed in 1966.

Sexual Orientation

There are four possible *sexual orientations*: heterosexual, homosexual, bisexual, and asexual. Seligman believes the gender of the sex partner about whom we fantasize reveals our true sexual disposition (1993,157). Although he has no data from research to support this assertion, it implies there can be difficulty in definitively ascertaining an individual's sexual orientation.

Further contributing to and complicating an understanding of sexual orientation is the American Psychiatric Association's removal of homosexuality as a disorder from the *Diagnostic and Statistical Manual* in 1973. Sigmund Freud would have approved of this decision since he did not see homosexuality as a disorder but a variation of sexual development. In a letter written to a mother who requested psychotherapy for her son Freud responded:

> Homosexuality is assuredly no advantage, but it is nothing to be ashamed of, no vice, no degradation, it cannot be classified as an illness; we consider it to be a variation of sexual function produced by a certain arrest of sexual development. … It is a great injustice to persecute homosexuality as a crime, and cruelty too (Freud, 1951, 786).

If the absence of a sex drive (asexuality) seems an impossibility, then consider Ben Barres, Chair of the Department of Neurobiology at Stanford University. Born Barbara Barres in 1955, he remained female until completing transsexual procedure in 1997. Most people have a sex drive and for some it is compelling. But a few, including Barres, have no such need. In an interview, he described himself as devoid of a sexual attraction to others and indifferent to sexual activity (2006).

Asexuality is not to be equated with celibacy. The former is disinterest in sexual activity; the latter is the choice to abstain from sexual relations in favor of a higher priority. In the *New Testament* the choice to forego sex is addressed both by the Apostle Paul and Jesus Christ. To the Corinthian Christians Paul wrote that celibacy is a gift given to some, including him, as part of a ministerial calling. He also wrote that if the need for sexual gratification is strong enough to distract from the work of ministry, then “it is better to marry than to burn with passion” (1 Corinthians 7:8, *New International Version*). Speaking to his disciples, Jesus said some people renounce marriage “for the kingdom of heaven” and others by nature have no sex drive (Matthew 19:12). Like Paul, he added that few are called to a celibate life: “Not everyone can accept this word, but only those to whom it has been given” (Matthew 19:11, *New International Version*).

Clearly, *sexual orientation* is not as simple a matter as some believe.

Sexual Preference

There are two organizations utilizing the acronym NAMBLA. One is the National Association of Marlon Brando Look Alikes and the other the North American Man Boy Love Association. (Both actually exist and, as the saying goes, "You can look it up.") The latter, with no support from the former, advocates for uncoerced pedophilia and pederasty as well as the decriminalization of sexual activity between adults and children when such engagements are consensual. To date the law deems these activities illegal; the American Psychiatric Association considers them pathological; and most people see them as reprehensible.

Sexual preference refers to the activities that provide arousal and gratification. The *Diagnostic and Statistical Manual IV* classifies pedophilia and seven other unusual sexual interests as psychosexual disorders, specifically *paraphilias* (which means attraction to the deviant). Psychologists Irwin and Barbara Sarason have described uncommon sexual interests in their textbook, *Abnormal Psychology*:

> Not everyone is sexually excited by the same stimuli. Some individuals gain satisfaction only from particular objects or situations. While many of these behaviors are practiced in private or with consenting adult partners and do not cause harm to other people, paraphilic imagery may be acted out with a non-consenting partner in a way that does cause harm (1996, 223).

The paraphilias found in the DSM – IV are characterized by one or more of three descriptions: (1) preference for the use of an object rather than a human partner for sexual arousal, (2) repetitive sexual activity with humans that involves real or simulated suffering or humiliation, or (3) repetitive sexual activity with non-consenting partners. The seven paraphilias determined by the American Psychiatric Association are:

Paraphilias	source of sexual excitement
exhibitionism	exposing genitalia (e.g. "flashers")
fetishism	object (e.g. undergarments or shoes)
frotteurism	sexually oriented touching of an unsuspecting person
pedophilia	prepubescent children
sexual masochism	suffering humiliation and pain
sexual sadism	inflicting humiliation and pain
transvestite fetishism	"cross-dressing"
voyeurism	spying on others (e.g. "peeping Toms")

It is simplistic to believe that *sexual preference* is simply a matter of any activity that provides sexual excitement and satisfaction is *ipso facto* healthy and normal.

Sexual Role

Concerning *sexual role*, there are three subcategories: *social, personality*, and *ability*. Expressed as questions, respectively, these differences are:

1. How does culture influence behavioral expectations for females and males?

2. Are there innate personality differences between males and females?

3. Are females naturally better than males at some tasks and vice versa?

Seligman has written, "Based on hundreds of studies and thousands of subjects ... there are huge sex-role differences between very young boys and girls" (1993, 165).

- By age two, boys want to play with trucks and girls want to play with dolls.
- By age three, children want to play with peers of their own sex.
- By age four, most girls want to be teachers, secretaries, and mothers; most boys want to have "masculine" jobs. (Maccoby and Jacklin, 1974).

However tempting it might be to attribute gender differences to parenting agendas and socialization, numerous studies show that children raised by parents who encouraged both male and female characteristics without favoring either are nonetheless stereotypically male and female.

> What is surprising is that kids reared androgynously retain their stereotypes as strongly as kids not so reared. Young kids' preferences bear no relationship to their parents' attitudes or their parents' education, class, employment, or sexual politics. Kids' play is strongly sex-stereotyped, regardless of their parents' attitudes or their parents' own sex-role behavior (1993, 165).

In the movie, "A League of Their Own," the male manager of a women's baseball team harshly criticizes one of his players. Incredulous when she breaks into tears, he asks her, "Are you crying?" and then informs her, "There's no crying in baseball" (1992). The setting of the movie is the

1940s, a time when women assumed many of the jobs previously held by men because of World War II. The implication of the "crying" scene in this movie is that women retain certain personality traits even when doing men's work. To be fair, it should be noted that neither Danica Patrick (autoracing driver) nor Lisa Kelly (ice-road trucker) has been reduced to tears doing their work. *Sexual role*, like identity, orientation, and preference, is not without its complications.

Sexual Performance

"When the time is right ..." begins a Cialis commercial. Cialis is an *erectile dysfunction* medication. *Erectile dysfunction,* often referred to simply as ED and a term unknown outside of medical circles a generation ago, is now familiar to most television watchers. The producers of Cialis, Viagra, and Levitra have brought to public attention the effectiveness of these medications for bringing a certain bodypart to prolonged attention. Sexual performance is the subcategory of sex concerned with how well a person functions "when the time is right."

Sexual dysfunctions run the full-range of performance possibilities: *frigidity* to *nymphomania, female orgasmic disorder* (inability to have an orgasm) to *persistent genital arousal disorder* (unwanted orgasms at the slightest stimulation), *anejaculation* (inability to ejaculate) to *premature ejaculation disorder*. It is peculiar that sexual performance, an activity that is integral to the perpetuation of our species, is subject to so many dysfunctions. (The same can be said about eating and its associated disorders.) Apparently sexual performance is more complicated than merely springing into action "when the time is right."

Concluding Thought

The premise of this book is the qualities that combine to make human beings unique also complicate the human situation, often creating predicaments. Arguably this is most evident when considering sex as part of the human condition.

12. What Is the Place of Love in the Human Predicament?

Love is an irresistible desire to be irresistibly desired.

- Robert Frost

Gravity is not responsible for people falling in love.

- Albert Einstein

One is very crazy when in love.

- Sigmund Freud

Love: poems idealize it; songs exaggerate it; novels romanticize it; movies dramatize it; and research analyzes it. It is recklessly pursued by some who fear they have missed it or will die without ever having known it. In his autobiography, philosopher Bertrand Russell revealed: "I have sought love, first, because it brings ecstasy – ecstasy so great that I would have sacrificed all the rest of life for a few hours of this joy (1975, 3).

Further, weddings celebrate it; separations reevaluate it; and divorces formalize its conclusion. In her essay, "Love and Hate in the Married State," Judith Viorst opined:

> We bring into marriage a host of romantic expectations. We may also bring visions of mythic sexual thrills. … We should achieve either paradise or a reasonable facsimile thereof. (Then) we adjust and compromise and make do, we sometimes hate the married state for domesticating our dreams of romantic love (1986, 188).

What is the place of love in the human situation? Like sex, with which it is often confused, it is a frequent contributor to the human predicament. Love is "an intense feeling of deep affection" (Morris, 1969, 772). Like God, true love is ineffable (beyond description) and immutable (unchangeable).

In contrast to English, Greek has four words for this vehement emotion: *storge, philia, eros*, and *agape*. *Storge* is "motherly love" - the natural flow of affection a mother has for her child. Clementina Geraci demonstrated this love when she was diagnosed with breast cancer and chose to forego the aggressive chemotherapy that would have aborted the baby developing within her. She opted for a less hazardous treatment and in her seventh month of pregnancy delivered a son by Caesarean section. Geraci, a medical doctor herself, died four months after her son's birth.

Philia is "friendship type love." It is experienced when people see something of themselves in another person and are attracted to that person. Philadelphia's nickname, "The City of Brotherly Love," is derived from *philia* and *adelphos* (brother). From its etymology, a *philosopher* is someone who has a friendship with wisdom (*sophos*).

Agape is the love of one person for another without sexual implications. It is the selfless, unconditional love of which Jesus spoke when he taught his disciples, "Greater love has no one than this, that he lay down his life for his friends" (John 15:13, *New International Version*). *Agape* is translated variously as "love" or "charity" in the New Testament in 1 Corinthians 13, the chapter often read in wedding ceremonies. Clementina Geraci is a real-life instantiation of *agape* as well as *storge*. A literary illustration of *agape* is found in the classic children's story *The Giving Tree*, written by Shel Silverstein (1964). Throughout the story the tree sacrificially gives to a little boy in the hope of making the boy happy. (Some have criticized *The Giving Tree* as a story of gratuitous giving that encourages enabling. Novelist and priest Father Andrew Greeley has cautioned parents against misguided, counterproductive acts of giving: "You can love [children] the wrong way perhaps, but you can't love them too much" (1983, 108).

Eros is love driven by the impulse to gratify the senses, especially sexual desire. In Greek mythology *Eros* is the son of Aphrodite and god of love. The adjective erotic is derived from *eros*, characterizing someone or something as sexually exciting. The poet Mary Karr denounced such love in "Reference for Ex-Man's Next," in which she berates an ex-boyfriend whose interest in her was exclusively sexual:

> ... vows you spout would fill a stadium empty as your chest ... pitched as underhand and low to schoolgirls you did con to bed – and yes, to me (2009, 33).

Love and Its Antithesis

One way to understand something is to consider its opposite. Love's antipode is narcissism. The term derives from Narcissus, the exceedingly handsome and self-absorbed character in Greek mythology who fell in love with his own reflection. Narcissism is an excessive self-love manifesting in extreme selfishness and a grandiose view of one's specialness.

Narcissistic personality disorder is one of ten personality disorders included in the *Diagnostic and Statistical Manual*. Its criminal expression, *antisocial personality disorder*, has the essential elements of narcissistic personality disorder with an additional attribute: the absence of a conscience. A Larry McMurtry novel features a character named Hud who fits this description (1961). In the book's movie version, he is told by his highly principled, God-fearing father, "You live only for yourself, and that makes you unfit to live with" (1963). Hud's life is antithetical to the "greater love" of which Jesus spoke and Clementina Geraci actualized.

An essential characteristic of love is a commitment to something greater than one's self. In his "I Have a Dream" speech the Reverend Dr. Martin Luther King, Jr. posited, "If a man has nothing to die for, then his life is not worth nothing" (1963). In a letter to his wife, a Civil War soldier named Sullivan Beaulieu expressed his recognition of something greater than himself and his willingness to die for it:

> If it is necessary that I should fall on the battlefield for my Country, I am ready. I have no misgivings about, or lack of confidence in, the cause in which I am engaged, and my courage does not halt or falter. I know how strongly American Civilization leans on the Government, and how great a debt we owe to those who went before us through the blood and sufferings of the Revolution. And I am willing – perfectly willing - to lay down all my joys in this life, to help maintain this Government, and to pay that debt … (Carroll, 1997, 111).

Beaulieu was killed at the First Battle of Bull Run one week after writing this letter.

Is love an evolutionary phenomenon?

Natural selection is "the principle that … those (traits) that lead to increased reproduction and survival will most likely be passed on to succeeding generations" (Myers, 2012, 139). Hence this question: *Does the capacity for love contribute to the reproduction and survival of the human species*?

> *Evolutionary psychology* is a theory of human behavior that incorporates the effects of evolution. As our

> ancestors confronted problems, they developed ways of solving those problems. Over time, the most successful solutions developed into basic instincts. We no longer need to consciously think about certain behaviors, as they simply "come naturally." Those behaviors are tempered by input from our culture, family, and individual factors, but the underlying behaviors are instinct (Fritscher, 2009).

An evolutionary psychologist might posit that the human ability to love is the result of an evolutionary process because love is integral to reproduction and survival. It is unlikely that this position is correct for at least three reasons. First, an advocate for this position would have to argue that love serves the purpose of mate attraction and commitment. Mate attraction and commitment are important because children are dependent beings many years longer than other animals and a two-parent family is optimal for child development. While a stable, two-parent family is ideal for children, attraction to someone other than a spouse can occur, threatening a family's stability.

Second, since sexual attraction can occur without love, the sex drive by itself is sufficient for impregnation and reproduction.

A third likely evolutionary argument is that love is the result of the highly developed human intellect, which has evolved to the extent that it can create pleasurable experiences through imagination. Love involves imagination when the beloved is absent and must be conceptualized in order to be enjoyed. And when the beloved is present, imagination can create enjoyable future possibilities. As far as is known, this is an exclusively human capability. However, there are many activities, some intellectual and others physical, that enrich life without contributing to species survival: writing novels and poetry, composing and listening to music, painting, sculpting, dancing, playing golf or tennis, and running marathons. Each of these activities appeals to one or more of the senses, thereby eliciting a pleasant experience. But none of them have ever have been necessary for reproduction and survival.

It is possible that love *indirectly* contributes to human preservation by being the emotional response to certain traits that *directly* contribute to reproduction and survival.

It is tenable that courage, helpfulness, kindness, industriousness, dependability, patience, and intelligence combined with a physical appearance that suggests good health and reproductive ability account for the desirable feeling of love. If this is true then love could be spoken of as an evolutionary phenomenon.

Concluding Thought

A popular song from many years ago asked, "What Is This Thing Called Love? (Porter, 1929). Whatever it is and however problematic it might be, it is undeniably a significant part of the human situation. Concerning love, the eminent anthropologist Helen Fisher has written:

> Romantic love. Obsessive love. Passionate love. Infatuation. Call it what you will, men and women of every era and culture have been "bewitched, bothered, and bewildered" by this irresistible power. Being in love is universal to humanity, it is part of human nature (2004, 6).

13. What Does It Mean to Be Religious?

Religion is intensive and comprehensive belief.

- Randolph Lumpp

Religion is the sigh of the oppressed, the heart of a heartless world, and the soul of soulless conditions. It is the opium of the people.

- Karl Marx

Sociologist Peter Berger has written, "If commentators on the contemporary situation of religion agree about anything, it is that the supernatural has departed from the modern world" (1969, 1). Notwithstanding, as implied by the title of his book, *A Rumor of Angels*, Berger believes a widespread fascination for the supernatural persists even in the current scientific age. Evidence of this fascination is the popularity of the movie, "The Sixth Sense." Written and directed by M. Night Shyamalan, its ticket sales exceeded production costs by $630,000,000 and it was America's number one box office attraction for five weeks in 1999. It is the story of an eight year-old boy who has the ability to peer into another dimension of reality and see dead people. The success of this movie is inexplicable apart from a widespread curiosity about preternatural activity. This same curiosity accounts for the immense popularity of Stephen King's novelistic excursions into a world that might be. Neurosurgeon Eben Alexander's recent memoir, *Proof of Heaven*, recounting his near-death experience, rose to the top of *The New York Times* paperback best-seller list immediately upon its publication (2012). Further, the popularity of astrology, which has no relationship with the science of astronomy, tarot card readings, seances, mediums, and other psychic activities provide additional support for Berger's assertion there is "a rumor of angels" among us.

The distinguished historian and philosopher Mircea Eliade believed human beings are hardwired for belief in the supernatural and employed the term *homo religiosus* (religious man) to characterize this disposition. In his classic, *The Sacred and the Profane*, he posited that all people, including those who claim to be exclusively secular in their worldview, are sometimes unconsciously attracted to sacred behaviors and beliefs (1987).

Not Religious, But Spiritual

Are human beings naturally disposed to pursue some form of faith in and worship of a supreme being? The celebrated humorist Will Rogers wryly said of himself, "I am not a member of any organized political party, I'm a democrat" (2012). Similarly, many people characterize themselves as "not religious, but spiritual." Like Rogers, such people have an interest without institutional membership. To be spiritual means to be dualistic - to believe there are two dimensions of reality, one physical and accessible by the senses, the other nonphysical and imperceptible to the senses. "Spirituality is a process that leads us on a journey from the seen to the unseen, the visible to the invisible dimension of human existence" (Ponomareff and Bryson, 2006, 89). Albert Einstein made a spiritual reference in a letter he wrote to a sixth grader who had written to ask if scientists pray. Einstein's response included this observation:

> ... everyone who is seriously involved in the pursuit of science becomes convinced that a spirit is manifest in the laws of the Universe – a spirit vastly superior to

> that of man and in the face of which we with our modest powers must feel humble (Calaprice, 2002)

Sigmund Freud and Carl Jung parted company largely because of their disagreement over the place of spirituality and religion in psychoanalysis. Freud, an atheist, dismissed the possibility of a spiritual realm. Jung not only subscribed to spiritual reality, but included it as part of the *collective unconscious* – the primitive man within all of us constituting "the common psychic heritage of us all" (Stevens, 1994, 7).

Freud explained human fascination with the supernatural and belief in God as primitive attempts to understand a perplexing world. He viewed prayer, baptism, and confession as ritualistic efforts to recruit a supernatural being's assistance in coping with life in a hostile environment. In one of his most controversial books, *The Future of an Illusion*, he characterized religion as an obsessive-compulsive neurosis:

> We know that a human child cannot successfully complete its development to the civilized stage without passing through a phase of neurosis ... In just the same way, one might assume, humanity as a whole, in its development through the ages, fell into stages analogous to neuroses, and for the same reasons – namely because of its ignorance and intellectual weakness ... Religion would thus be the universal obsessional neurosis of humanity; like the obsessional neurosis of children ...If this view is right, it is to be supposed that a turning away from religion is bound to occur with the fatal inevitability of a process of growth (1961, 70-71).

Being Freud's intellectual adversary, Jung would have appreciated an experiment conducted by Professor Bruce Hood at Bristol University in 2006. Hood demonstrated the human tendency to associate an inexplicable power with certain objects. In his experiment he offered his students ten pounds (approximately sixteen dollars) to wear a cardigan sweater. After first agreeing to wear the sweater, almost all of them refused when they were told it once belonged to Fred West, an infamous serial murderer. Interesting is that the students who changed their mind were unable to explain why. Hood believes we are hard-wired to consider the possibility of supernatural powers in addition to our receptivity to scientific explanations.

Why religion?

William James defined religion as, "an attempt to be in harmony with an unseen order of things" (Peck, 1993, 233). What human needs are addressed, if not satisfied, by the pursuit of a religious life? The ethnocentric argument for the existence of God posits that all cultures across human history have demonstrated some form of religion. (This is not to say that all people within a given culture are or have been religious. Neither is this to say that all religions are essentially the same.) The ethnocentric argument points to four metaphysical curiosities shared by all human beings:

1. We are curious about the origin of the universe. Since nothing can be the cause of itself, we wonder if the cosmos is eternal or if it owes its existence to a prior entity – possibly a supernatural, eternal being.

2. We have a curiosity about the possibility of God's existence, if only to reject such a notion.

3. We have a curiosity about death. Like Hamlet, we ponder the afterlife possibilities without certainty as to our ultimate state.

4. At least intellectually, we recognize the problem of moral relativity. Dostoevsky's Ivan Karamazov proposed that if God does not exist there is no standard against which to evaluate human conduct. Hence, each culture would be its own moral authority. And if this is the case, then neither slavery nor the Holocaust is immoral.

These four curiosities cannot be investigated scientifically. They are philosophical issues – the first three are metaphysical and the last is ethical. Religion addresses all four of these topics. Science is limited in its pursuit of knowledge; but this does not mean the pursuit of knowledge is limited to science. Freud maintained a simplistic confidence in science:

> The riddles of the universe reveal themselves only slowly to our investigation; there are many questions to which science today can give no answer. But scientific work is the only road which can lead us to a knowledge of reality outside ourselves (1927, 50).

In contrast to Freud, Berger has written approvingly of the willingness to entertain supernatural explanations: "A rediscovery of the supernatural will be, above all, a regaining of openness in our perception of reality" (1969, 95).

14. How Do We Experience Pleasure?

The psychologist Paul Rozin points out that if you look through a psychology textbook, you will find little or nothing about sports, art, music, drama, literature, play, and religion. These are central to what makes us human, and we won't understand any of them until we understand pleasure.

- Paul Bloom

We call things beautiful when experience of them gives us a particular kind of pleasure. It is a sense that they are as they should be, that there is something exactly right about them.

- Simon Blackburn

Henry Murray, a distinguished psychology professor at Harvard for over thirty years, identified twenty-seven psychological needs that energize and direct human behavior. His list includes *sentience*, the motivation to experience sensual pleasure; to have an encounter that is pleasing to see, hear, feel, smell or taste.

Psychologists are not alone in their interest in sentience. One of the six subcategories of philosophy, *aesthetics*, "refers to those things that are pleasing to the senses; beautiful to see or hear. The aesthetic questions are: What makes someone or something aesthetically pleasing? How is beauty determined? What constitutes a work of art or a classic?" (Malikow, 2009, xi). In his *Meditations*, Rene Descartes offered "Je pense donc je suis" ("I think, therefore, I am") as the foundation of knowledge (1999, xxviii). According to Descartes, by virtue of thinking people have assurance of their existence. However, certainty of existence is not enough for a meaningful life. People require the experience of pleasure and seek out events and activities they believe will provide it. [The desire for pleasure can be so strong that it can suspend good judgment.] The extramarital dalliances of King David, President Clinton, and countless lesser lights through the ages demonstrate the need for enjoyment can lead to ethical misconduct and engagement in self-indulgent, high risk behavior.

Of course, not all pleasure seeking is morally questionable and/or imprudent. Breathtaking sunsets and the splendor of the Grand Canyon are magnificent to see. Whether it is Handel's "Messiah" or Kenny Rogers' "The Gambler," certain arrangements of sounds are pleasing, if not moving, to hear. A television commercial asks, "Do you dream in chocolate?" implying some tastes are so delightful they cannot be contained to waking hours. Shakespeare's Juliet reminds us that an aroma can be delightful: "What's in a name? That which we call a rose by any other name would smell as sweet" (1597, Act II, Scene 2). And Romeo, gazing at Juliet, ponders the delight of a certain touch: "See how she leans her cheek upon her hand! O that I were a glove upon that hand. That I might touch that cheek." (1597, Act II, Scene 2).

Psychological Set

Experiencing pleasure is easier than explaining it.

On the morning of January 12, 2007, a young man in jeans, a long-sleeved T-shirt, and baseball cap walked into a Washington subway station and pulled out a violin. He laid out his violin case in front of him, seeded it with a few dollars and some change, and then played six classical pieces for the next 43 minutes, as over a thousand people walked by.

> This was no ordinary street performer. He was Joshua Bell, one of the world's great violinists, and he was playing his $3.5 million violin, handcrafted in 1713 by Antonio Strativari. A few nights before, Bell performed at Boston's Symphony Hall. Now he stood in front of commuters playing for coins. This was an experiment by Gene Weingarten, a reporter for the Washington Post. It was intended as an "unblinking assessment of public taste": how would people respond to great art in a mundane context, when nobody was telling them how great it was?
>
> The people failed. Over a thousand commuters passed, and Bell netted a bit over $32. Not bad, but nothing special. The commuters were indifferent to what they were hearing (Bloom, 2010, 117-118).

In defense of the commuters, perhaps they were in an early morning rush and too preoccupied to be drawn to the artistry in their midst. Notwithstanding, why wasn't the beauty of Bell's performance adequate to redirect their attention? Certainly, not all of the commuters were either tone deaf or musically disinterested. A more likely explanation is *psychological set* – the predisposition to react to a stimulus in a certain way. Psychological set is the state of mind that influences perception. It seems that Joshua Bell is experienced differently depending on where he is heard – a concert hall or a subway station. (Interesting is that Bell said the only people who stopped to listen were children until they were moved along by the adults tending them.)

The experience of smell also is influenced by psychological set. In a study conducted by Rachel Herz of Brown University a group of subjects were blindfolded and asked to describe the small of the cheese that would be placed under their nose. A second group, also blindfolded, was asked to describe the bowl of vomit that would be placed under their nose. The second group was not told the truth. Like the first group, they would be smelling cheese. Most of the second group subjects became nauseous and some of them vomited (Ross, 2013).

Yale psychologist Paul Bloom reports, "There have been several studies showing that how you think about food or drink affects how you judge it" (2010, 45). In How Pleasure Works, he offers these results:

> ... protein bars taste worse if they are described as "soy protein;" orange juice tastes better if it is bright orange; children think milk and apples taste better if they're taken out from McDonald's bags; Coke is rated higher when drunk from a cup with a brand logo (45).

Such findings give credibility to a scene in the movie "The Prince of Tides" in which an unsuspecting man compliments his wife on the special dinner she's prepared for him – a plate of fried dog food (1991).

Even the experience from touch is subject to psychological set. If people were blindfolded and stroked the backs of a rabbit, cat, and rat it is unlikely they could distinguish one from another. However, it is probable their experience would be influenced if they knew which animal they were petting. (This hypothesis has not been experimentally tested.)

Psychological set offers a partial explanation for the art world's change of mind when seeing a Vincent van Gogh painting.

> It is remarkable that a Van Gogh painting ("Sunflowers") that did not have a single buyer during the artist's lifetime was sold at auction for 39.9 million dollars in 1987. What change of conditions accounts for a painting going from worthless to virtually priceless? Art collectors in Van Gogh's day saw the same

> images and colors on canvas seen by contemporary art collectors. Yet, the perceptions of the two groups are very different (Malikow, 2009, 24).

Whether it is hearing, smelling, tasting, seeing, or touching, "sensation is always colored by our beliefs" (Bloom, 2010, 49).

Is beauty "out there" or "in here?"

Philosophy's best known conundrum, "If a tree falls in the forest and there's no one there to hear it, is there a noise?" can be adapted to the question of beauty, "If a sunset occurs and there's no one looking at it, is it nevertheless beautiful?" In other words, is beauty in the object or eye of the beholder? If the latter, then in the absence of a beholder there can be no beauty. Philosophers like G.E. Moore, who take a "common sense" approach to such questions, would maintain that beauty is in the object. Since experience teaches us that falling trees make noise and sunsets are beautiful, it follows that beauty exists independently of any number of observers. Just as a right triangle has a 90 degree angle whether or not anyone is observing it, so also sunsets and other objects have inherent characteristics. A sunset is no more beautiful if a hundred people are observing it rather than ten. And that same sunset would be no less beautiful if it had only one observer. By logical extension, the sunset retains all of its characteristics, including beauty, even if no one is experiencing it.

Those who would agree with Moore are not without opposition. The eighteenth century British philosopher David Hume expressed a *sentimentalist* view of ethics with these words: "Morals excite passions, and produce or prevent actions. Reason itself is utterly impotent in this particular. The rules of morality, therefore, are not conclusions of our reason" (1967, 325). Applying sentimentalism to aesthetics results in the conclusion that beauty is *not* a characteristic of the object being observed. Rather, beauty is an experience of the observers. Hence, if there are no observers, there is no beauty. For the sentimentalist, beauty is "out there" (among the observers), not "in here" (inherent to the object). For the sentimentalist, nothing is inherently beautiful; people simply *feel* a certain way about some things. According to the sentimentalist falling trees in an uninhabited forest do not make noise and unobserved sunsets have no beauty.

Still, if the sentimentalist is correct, then why are there some things, like sunsets, that evoke the same feeling in almost everyone? On the other hand, if there is such a thing as inherent beauty, then why does beauty vary among cultures as well as within the same culture across time? These questions were addressed by Immanuel Kant's *antinomy of taste.*

The Antinomy of Taste

An *antinomy* is encountered when two propositions that are considered together cannot both be true, but when considered separately both seem to be true. A more familiar term carrying the same meaning is *paradox,* a statement that seems self-contradictory but, nevertheless, might be true. This appears to be the case in the enduring debate over free will and determinism. Advocates for free will maintain that people engage in authentic choice-making and are responsible for the consequences that emanate from their choices. Determinists counter that the *law of cause-and-effect* renders free will an illusion, thereby negating responsibility. When considered together, these propositions are irreconcilable and seem to force an "either/or" decision. However, when considered separately, each seems to be supported by valid reasoning, experience, and common sense. The same apparent incompatibility is observed in Immanuel Kant's *antinomy of taste.*

De gustibus non est disputandum (taste is not to be disputed) is an appealing motto until an argument erupts over a work of art, interior design, contestants in a beauty pageant, or entrants in a pie contest. When we are engaged in such disputes,

> We regard the other as badly tuned, and contend for our own way of looking at things. That implies we are prepared to insist on a standard: in our thoughts there is after all such a thing as good taste, as educated judgment or even as being objectively right or wrong. So it seems that we oscillate between pure subjectivity (de gustibus …) and at least a degree of objectivity (Blackburn, 2009, 152).

Which proposition concerning taste is true? Does the adage, "There's no accounting for taste" conclude the matter? If so, there's no accounting for a literary, musical, or theatrical classic. This would mean the term classic is *meaningless*. But this is not the case. Classics are those creative works that have passed the test of time (at least two generations), demonstrated transcultural appeal, and achieved recognition as extraordinary by the appropriate experts. The standard for status as a classic is tripartite: *temporality, universality*, and *authority*.

"How then are we to reconcile the two sides of Kant's antinomy or paradox?" (Blackburn, 2009, 153). Like Robin Williams' character, Mr. Keating, in the movie "Dead Poets Society," Kant believed an individual's experience of a poem, book, symphony, play or movie constitutes a significant subjective statement. As well, when people from different eras and cultures agree with those who have refined taste, a substantial objective statement has been made. There is no "either/or" decision to be made when an aggregate of subjective experiences converge with collective expert opinion. Individuals can describe *what* they felt when experiencing a creative work; scholars can explain *why* that feeling occurred. However, no description of an object or event is adequate to evoke a pleasurable sensation in a non-experiencer.

> If someone tells me that a garden or a painting or a wedding was beautiful, but I was not there, then all I can properly say is that I heard it was beautiful (154).

Kant conceded, "There can be no rule according to which anyone is able to be compelled to recognize something as beautiful" (1952, 56). But this does not mean there are no standards for assessing an artistic work. Hume wrote favorably of the critic who has a "delicate discrimination" and "practised eye" (1985, 1, 23).

A mediating statement between pure subjectivity and pure objectivity is found in Kant's definition of *aesthetic*:

> By an aesthetic idea I mean that representation of the imagination which induces much thought, yet without the possibility of any definite thought whatever being adequate to it (1952, 144).

While we might be disappointed when someone else does not share our wonder at the Grand Canyon or "Les Miserables," it is the person who seems unable to marvel at anything who is puzzling and troubling to us.

> The man that has no music in himself
> Nor is moved with concord of sweet sounds
> Is fit for treasons, strategems and spoils;
> The motions of his spirit are as dull as night,
> And affections as dark as Erebus:
> Let no such man be trusted
> (Shakespeare, The Merchant of Venice, Act I, scene 1).

An Experience with Beauty: Meeting Amy Mullins

Herman Hesse has written of the road that leads a man to himself. For the man in this story an unplanned encounter in a tavern seems to have paved such a road. Imagine a man sitting at a bar, taking his last sip of Chardonnay before leaving when a stunning woman takes the seat next to him. Without staring, he sizes her up as late-twenties, impeccably dressed with shoulder-length, perfectly coiffed blond hair, a flawless complexion more like porcelain than skin, and mesmerizing blue eyes. Knowing he'll regret not even trying, he begins a conversation and is delighted by her friendliness. More than that, as if more was necessary to rivet his attention, he finds her pleasantly articulate. Over the next hour, from a series of questions designed to keep the conversation going, he learns that she's a Georgetown University graduate where she competed in track-and-field and currently working as an actress and model when not involved in several not-for-profit organizations.

She glances at her watch (fortunately for the first time) and says, "I have an early flight to catch in the morning, I better be going." In synchrony, they rise, extend right hands, and say "Nice to meet you." Emboldened by this serendipitous choreography, he asks for her phone number. As though she expected the question - of course she did, she gets it all the time - she gives him her card, instructing him to use the cell number when he calls.

She leaves without looking back but his eyes never leave her. Returning home with an excitement that precludes falling asleep, he fires up his PC, ostensibly to check for e-mails. Almost immediately he switches to *Google* and mindlessly types in, "Aimee Mullins." In less than a second, the first wave of over 500,000 results appears. After ten minutes of reading he has learned much: She attended Georgetown on a full academic scholarship, one of three awarded by the Department of Defense, graduating with honors from the School of Foreign Service. At seventeen, Aimee was the youngest person ever to hold top-security clearance at the Pentagon, where she worked summers as an intelligence analyst. In 1999 she made her debut as a runway model in London at the invitation of Alexander McQueen, an internationally renown fashion designer. She's appeared in *Vogue, Harper's Bazaar*, and *Elle*. In addition, she was in *Esquire's* "Women We Love" issue, *People Magazine* as one of the "50 Most Beautiful People," and on *Rolling Stone's* "Annual Hot List." Aimee also had the starring role in a highly acclaimed film, "Cremaster 3." She mentioned she's an athlete - that was an understatement. She's featured in exhibits in the NCAA Hall of Fame and Track and Field Hall of Fame and acclaimed in *Sports Illustrated* as one of the "Coolest Women in Sport." At this point he's hardly surprised when reading that the Women's Museum in Dallas, Texas honored her as one of the "Greatest Women of the 20th Century" for her achievements in sports.

The surprise came when he learned that Aimee Mullins is a double amputee! Born without shinbones, both her legs were amputated below the knee when she was a year-old. Her parents decided life with prosthetics would provide her with more mobility than life in a wheelchair. She was born with *fibular hemimelia*, a congenital condition in which large bones in the extremities are absent - a condition that usually occurs in one limb and more often among boys.

More accurately, his reaction was one of shock, not surprise. He had never heard of this condition and there was nothing in Aimee's gait that suggested even an ankle sprain let alone prosthetic legs under her Cynthia Vincent full-length skirt. A cascade of questions followed: Am I still going to call her? If not, why? Why should "no legs" make a difference? Doesn't this make her all the more impressive? If I do call, how do I bring up what I've learned? ("Oh, I looked you up in *Wikipedia* and learned you're from Allentown, Pennsylvania and that you don't have legs - I mean, real ones.") If I don't call, she'll know why. How can I hurt her by not calling?

He then realized that this is about him, not her. He wondered, "Is it that I don't want to hurt her or that I don't want to generate evidence of my shallowness? And if I do call, would it be to reassure myself that I'm not superficial? After all, she gave me her number, I'm the one wrestling with how to proceed."

More self-examination followed: "Why do I need to date a perfect woman? Isn't that what I thought Aimee was until I learned about her disability? How can I even think of her as disabled? Would she be more accomplished if she had legs? And, what if she had legs but was vain and narcissistic with nothing in her biography but a long history of suitors? Would that make her more desirable?"

Postscript

The preceding thought experiment raises several questions concerning the relative value of human characteristics. What are the qualities that make a person appealing and worthy of admiration and acclaim? Does Aimee have these qualities? Should her so-called disability discourage a prospective suitor? If so, why? The sardonic adage "Heroes are not born, they are cornered," implies that acts of extraordinary courage result from situations in which there is no choice but to act heroically. Aimee Mullins did not choose to be born with fibular hemimelia, neither did she make the decision for a double amputation. However, throughout her life, she has repeatedly chosen to pursue her interests and test her limits. Is she courageous? Another adage teaches that "Determinism is the hand we've been dealt, free will is the choice of how that hand is played." Aimee Mullins has chosen to "play her hand" by living life to the fullest, challenging and inspiring others to do the same. Is she heroic?

Her resiliency is reminiscent of Dax Cowart, who in 1973 was severely burned in an automobile explosion. In the accident he lost two-thirds of his skin, both hands, both eyes, and both ears. He attempted suicide several times and his appeals to have medical treatment discontinued were denied. Eventually, he accepted his lot as "The Man Sentenced to Life," graduated from law school, and married (Wicker, 1989). Like Aimee Mullins, his recovery from misfortune is remarkable.

Aimee has said, "The only true disability is a crushed spirit" (Lafave, 2010). Certainly she has displayed determination in addition to a host of other favorable qualities: confidence, compassion, intelligence, resilience, and self-discipline. She also has a sense of humor: "Interesting, from an identity standpoint, what does it mean to have a disability? Pamela Anderson has more prosthetics in her body than I do and nobody calls her disabled" (Mullins, 2009). In this age of cosmetic procedures, it is reasonable to ask why artificial legs would be considered unattractive. No doubt, for some men Aimee's admirable traits would not offset what she's lacking below the knee. For others, her prosthetics would be a non-issue. Apparently the author Salman Rushdie is in the latter category; the sixty year-old author and Aimee have been in a relationship for several years.

This thought experiment provides an opportunity to consider some of the 17,953 traits that contribute to personality (Allport, 1936). Moreover, it provides an opportunity to reflect upon what makes someone not only aesthetically appealing, but truly attractive.

15. Should We Never Give Up on a Dream?

Sometimes we have to give up the life we've planned to have the life that's waiting for us.

- Anonymous

Our deepest tragedy ... is not the tragedy of failing to realize our dream, but that of not even having a dream.

- David Elton Trueblood

I have a dream.

- M.L. King, Jr.

Augusten Burroughs believes some dreams need to be abandoned:

> Every time I watch some trembling, weepy girl stand at the podium to accept her best female pop vocal performance Grammy and start thanking her ICM agent and God, I cringe because I know what's next. "And I just want to say to every little girl out there watching tonight, listen to me: never, never give up your dream. If your dream is to stand here where I am, you don't let anybody stop you. And I promise, someday the world will be watching you up here."
>
> I just want to ask one of these singers, have you ever watched a single one of the many thousands of abysmal covers of your own song that are on YouTube? Because those are dreams. Dreams are not always beautiful things.

> I know these Grammy winners in their spaghetti strap gowns mean well but there are many, many people who do not need to be told to cling to their dreams; they need to have those dreams wrenched from their little fists before they waste their entire lives trying to achieve them. (2012, 145-146).

Similarly, psychotherapist Judith Viorst has written favorably about giving up on some dreams:

> For the road to human development is paved with renunciations. Throughout our life we grow by giving up. We give up some of our deepest attachments to others. We give up certain cherished parts of ourselves. We must confront, in the dreams we dream, as well as in our intimate relationships, all that we never will have and never will be. Passionate investment leaves us vulnerable to loss. And sometimes, no matter how clever we are, we must lose. (1986, 16).

Burroughs provocative humor and Viorst's eloquence notwithstanding, do we not need dreams? Robert Browning poetically expressed the necessity of dreams when he wrote: "Ah, but a man's reach should exceed his grasp, or what's a heaven for?" (1855).

Dreams that Came True

Daniel Eugene Reuttiger, immortalized by the movie "Rudy," was an unrecruited, non-scholarship ("walk-on") football player who achieved his goal of playing for the University of Notre Dame. His determination compensated for his mediocre academic and athletic abilities. To fulfill his childhood dream "Rudy" had to disregard the unanimous opinion of family and friends that he was pursuing the impossible.

Another highly motivated, minimally skilled athlete is Rocky Balboa, who captured professional boxing's most coveted title: heavyweight champion of the world. However, since Rocky is fictional the movie bearing his name might not be a reliable source of inspiration (1976). But James Braddock is real and his ascendancy to the heavyweight title is accurately recounted in the movie, "The Cinderella Man" (2005). In 1935 he went from relying on public assistance to supporting his family as the heavyweight champion of the world.

Yet another movie, a documentary titled "King Gimp," chronicles the life of Dan Keplinger, an accomplished artist with cerebral palsy so severe that he is continuously experiencing muscle spasms in one or another part of his body. When majoring in art at Towson State University in Maryland, one of the art professors refused to work with him, believing it would be impossible for Keplinger to accomplish all the projects required of art majors. Keplinger believes, "Obstacles and challenges are a part of the human condition. We all face them in everyday life, however we also have a choice as to how to deal with them." (Leibs, 2009).

Another remarkable dream pursuer and accomplisher is David Hartman, M.D. In 1976 he became the first blind person to earn a medical degree. Dr. Hartman was rejected by nine medical schools before being accepted by Temple University. Now 62 years-old and a practicing psychiatrist, he believes, "Everyone is handicapped in some way" (Hartman, 1976).

Dreams that Did Not Come True

Rudyard Kipling wrote, "If you can dream and not make dreams your master" (2002). As with anything in which there is emotional investment, wisdom is required if dreamers are to be masters, rather than servants, of their dreams. The British explorer Ernest Shackleton exemplifies this principle. In 1914 he abandoned his dream of being the first explorer to transverse Antarctica when his ship sank in the Weddell Sea. His dream yielded to the goal of getting twenty-seven men home safely. This required an 800 mile expedition in one of the world's most hostile environments. Often traveling no more than two miles a day, Shackleton and his entire crew survived the journey.

The problem with locating true stories of people who wisely abandoned a dream is that they rarely write a memoir or become the subject of a biography, movie or documentary. Instead they are the people who settle into a relatively ordinary life as compared to the life of which they dreamed. Archibald “Moonlight” Graham is one such person. In 1905 he played one inning of major league baseball without even once getting up to bat. At the season's end, rather than return to the minor leagues, he enrolled in medical school and following graduation practiced forty-four years in Chisholm, Minnesota. (Although a real person, Graham is featured in the fictional movie “Field of Dreams.”)

There is something instructive in Graham's odyssey. He went as far as he could in pursuit of his dream, realized he would get no closer, and fastened upon another dream. Pete Gray, a one-armed baseball player, had a longer major league career than Graham. Gray played a full season with the St. Luis Browns in 1945. Another improbable major leaguer is Jim Abbott, a pitcher born with one hand who played ten years in the big leagues, winning 87 games, one of them a no-hitter. Gray and Abbott, against all odds, progressed through amateur and minor league baseball, succeeding at each level. Eventually, their incremental success placed them in the major leagues. Others, like Graham and Pete Naton, gave themselves a deadline for fulfilling their dream. Naton was signed in 1953 by the Pittsburgh Pirates after graduating from Holy Cross College. He immediately went to the major leagues for a brief stint, appearing in six games. He was then sent to the minor leagues and made progress in the Pittsburgh minor league system without returning to the Pirates. Naton had predetermined that if he did not return to the major leagues by the time he became a father, he would retire from baseball. In 1958 he left baseball for a successful career in sales.

How to Decide

The encouraging adage, "What would you do if you did not have to worry about failure?" speaks to pursuing a dream without any instruction as to when to abandon that dream. No doubt there are dreams that would have come true had they not been forsaken. Notwithstanding, some dreams should be relinquished. The challenge is knowing when to discontinue the chase. "Moonlight" Graham gave himself a deadline based on another interest – medicine. Pete Naton's deadline was determined by his responsibility to his family. Ernest Shackleton was redirected by his obligation to his crew.

John Greenlief Whittier wrote, "For all sad words of tongue or pen. The saddest are these: 'It might have been!'" (1897). If there exists an alternate universe that includes those things that "might have been," there is no human access to it. Rudyard Kipling's poem, "If," offers a reliable guiding principle for the abdication of a dream:

> If you can trust yourself when all men doubt you,
> But make allowance for their doubting too. ...
> If you can dream – and not make dreams your master;
> If you can think – and not make thoughts your aim (2002).

The poet suggests a balanced approach to dream pursuit. The doubts of others should influence our thinking without being the determining factor. Dreams can provide direction, but no one should be mastered by a dream. Every dreamer should acknowledge: “I am the master of my fate and the captain of my soul” (Henley, 2003).

Cognitive Questions: How We Know and Think

16. What Does It Mean to be a *Homo Sapien*?

Drinking when we are not thirsty and making love all year round, madam, that is all there is to distinguish us from other animals.

- Pierre-Augusten Caron Beaumarchais, The Marriage of Figaro

For with much wisdom comes much sorrow; the more knowledge, the more grief.

- Ecclesiastes 1:18

An earlier version of human beings is *homo erectus*, so named because these were men (*homo*) who walked upright (*erectus*). The current humanoid model, to which we belong, is homo sapien, so named because of our ability to be rational and exercise wisdom (*sapien*). The assertion that drinking when not thirsty and year round love making are the only two features that distinguish us from other animals is simplistic. The abilities to learn, create, represent symbolically, experience shame, and have self-awareness contribute to an impressive list of capacities unique to human beings. Unfortunately, each of these favorable capabilities carries with it at least one undesirable possibility.

Learning

A colloquial definition of learning is, "the ongoing effort to make sense of experiences." A formal definition is, "any experience that results in a relatively permanent change in behavior" (Malikow, 2006, 2). Both definitions are applicable to the "Ten Foods Exercise." Consider the following list:

1. broccoli
2. blueberries
3. garlic
4. green tea
5. nuts
6. oats
7. red wine
8. salmon
9. spinach
10. tomatoes

Other than the obvious answer that this is a list of things to eat or drink, what is this list? Attempting to answer this question requires an effort to make sense of why these foods are grouped together. If you determined it is a list of healthy foods then you are correct. In fact, it is a list of the ten foods most nutritionists agree should be included in a healthy diet (Horowitz, 2003, 50-55). (They also agree that French fries should be eliminated from everyone's diet. Sorry about this.)

In addition to making sense of this list, did you learn anything? If the mere acquisition of information constitutes learning and if this information was new to you then learning has occurred. However, a more ambitious understanding of learning includes behavioral change. Defined in this way learning has not occurred unless at least some of these foods are integrated into your diet. Certainly the ability to learn is good. However, frustration can result from failed attempts at behavioral change. In the New Testament, the Apostle Paul described disappointment in himself for not behaving as he knew he should: "I do not understand what I do. For what I want to do I do not do. But what I hate I do. … What a wretched man I am!" (Romans 7:15, 24, *New International Version*).

The renown psychiatrist Scott Peck confessed to smoking, drinking, and serial adultery – all against his better judgment. Like Paul, he admitted to an irrational part of himself that frequently overpowered the part of himself that knew better (1995, 28-30). Peck unhappily concluded, "I always wished I could have been a different kind of person" (28).

Another frustration associated with learning is forgetting. Memory lapses are especially upsetting to older adults who tend to experience forgetting as a betrayal of the mind. Billy Collins well described these failures to recall in his poem "Forgetfulness" (2001, 29).

> The name of the author is the first to go followed obediently by the title, the plot the heartbreaking conclusion, the entire novel which suddenly becomes one you have never read, never even heard of, as if, one by one, the memories you used to harbor decided to retire to the southern hemisphere of the brain, to a little fishing village where there are no phones ...Whatever it is you are struggling to remember, it is not poised on the tip of your tongue, not even lurking in some obscure corner of your spleen ...
>
> No wonder you rise up in the middle of the night to look up the date of a famous battle in a book on war.
>
> No wonder the moon in the window seems to have drifted out of a love poem that you used to know by heart.

Creativity

The reorganization of words results in books, plays, poems, and movie scripts. The rearrangement of musical notes produces songs and symphonies. The reconfiguration of clay, paint, and plaster generates works of art. Creativity is the ability to bring something new into being from preexisting material. When creativity is flowing, excitement and satisfaction are experienced by the artist. However, when it is not, frustration is the artist's lot. It is generally accepted that the celebrated novelist Ernest Hemingway committed suicide when he was no longer able to write. (Alcoholism, depression, and other maladies account for his unremitting "writer's block.")

In addition, with the blessing of creativity comes the curse of imagining future misfortunes and recreating past unpleasantries. The mind's ability to move forward and backward in time can generate anxiety as well as psychosomatic conditions. Neurobiologist Robert Sapolsky's intriguingly titled book, *Why Zebras Don't Get Ulcers*, explains that animals are exempt from these uniquely human maladies because they cannot conceptualize anxiety producing scenarios. Neither can they reflect on the past and regret bad behavior or missed opportunities. Late in life the British journalist Malcolm Muggeridge wrote:

> The saddest thing to me, in looking back on my life, has been to recall, not so much the wickedness I have been involved in, the cruel and selfish and egoistic things I have done, the hurt I have inflicted on those I loved – although all that is painful enough. What hurts most is the preference I have so often shown for what is inferior, tenth rate, when the first rate was there for the having. Like a man who goes shopping and comes back with cardboard shoes when he might have had leather, with dried fruit when he might have had fresh, with processed cheese when he might have had cheddar, with paper flowers when the primroses were out (Hunter, 1998, 258).

Symbolic Representation

A simple experiment: point out something to a dog. Result: the dog will *not* look at the object at which you are pointing but will at your finger or mouth (if it's moving). The reason for this is that a dog is incapable of *symbolic representation*, a term used by the renown Swiss psychologist Jean Piaget to characterize that stage of a child's development at which one thing is indicative of something other than itself. It is indeed remarkable that the symbol sequence "C – A – T" corresponds to the sound "KAT" as well as the house pet that purrs, pursues mice, and meows.

Symbolic representation signals drivers to stop at intersections (red lights and octagonal red signs) and warns pedestrians of wet, slippery floors (yellow signs with a skidding figure). Vincent van Gogh and Claude Monet beautifully communicated symbolic representations of the world as they saw it. Albert Einstein symbolically represented the motion of objects in space using numbers configured in elaborate formulas.

How could there be a collateral liability with such a marvelous asset? Anyone with a learning disability could easily answer that question. The simple "C – A – T" progression is not immediately decipherable to many who have dyslexia. Just as red lights and algebraic formulas are sources of frustration, respectively, for those who are color-blind and "math-phobic."

Experience Guilt and Shame

The difference between guilt and shame is the former is feeling sorry for something we have done; the latter is being sorry for who we are. Psychologist Henry Murray included the need to avoid humiliation (*shame-avoidance*) in his list of twenty-seven fundamental human needs (1938).

Herein lies the positive feature of the ability to experience guilt and shame. It influences behavior toward conformity to a moral code – cultural and/or personal. As previously noted, Viktor Frankl posited the experience of guilt serves a good purpose when it results in a recommitment to living life as one believes it ought to be lived.

Unfortunately, guilt can gestate, be born as shame, and culminate as suicide. In his landmark study of suicide, the French sociologist Emile Durkheim included *anomic suicide* as one of four categories of self-enacted death. *Anomic suicides* are those in which the deceased was in a state of moral disorder owing to a dramatic social change or personal moral failure. Mark Twain wrote, "Man is the only animal that blushes. Or needs to" (1970, 1). It is one thing to blush; it is quite another to address humiliation by accomplishing suicide.

Experience Self-Awareness

Ayn Rand wrote, "To say 'I love you' one must first be able to say the 'I'" (2013). The psychological term for the ability to "say the 'I'" is *self-awareness*. In addition to thinking, acting, and experiencing we *think about* our thoughts, actions, and feelings in addition to recognizing them as our own. This ability to look inside ourselves is the introspection Socrates had in mind when he said, "The unexamined life is not worth living" (Plato, 399 B.C.). Self-awareness further means the ability to recognize ourselves as individuals who are separate and distinct from other people and our environment. Without self-awareness we would be incapable of managing our lives.

Nevertheless, there is a downside to self-awareness. The late David Foster Wallace described it as "our default setting, hardwired into our boards at birth" (2009, 38). He cautioned that this capacity, although natural, can sabotage relationships.

> Think about it: There is no experience you've had that you were not at the absolute center of. Everything in my own immediate experience supports my deep feeling that I am the absolute center of the universe, the realest, most vivid and important person in existence. We rarely think about this sort of natural, basic self-centeredness, because it's so socially repulsive, but it's pretty much the same for all of us, deep down (36-37).

Empathy is the competency to identify the emotional state of another person and respond appropriately. It is the ability to become another person, to a certain extent, for a little while and it is integral to interpersonal relationships. In Chaim Potok's novel, *The Chosen*, a father recognizes his young son's self-absorption and lack of empathy. The father takes the questionable action of raising his son in silence; speaking with him only when studying the *Torah* and *Talmud* – the Jewish holy books. The son's confusion and pain have the effect of nurturing empathy in the way Betty Sue Flowers described the process: "Pain is a mechanism for growth. It carves out the heart and allows more room for compassion" (Cronkite, 1994, 325).

Without a virtue to counterbalance it, self-awareness is a defect. The Scottish psychiatrist R.D. Laing understood this and wrote:

> My self-being, my consciousness and feeling of myself, that taste of myself, of *I* and *me* above and in all things, includes my taste of you. I taste you and you taste me. … It is difficult to understand the *self-being*

> of the other. I cannot experience it directly. I must rely on the other's actions and testimony to infer how he experiences himself (1969, 35).

The ability to communicate provides the counterbalancing virtue. Still, acquiring the "self-being of the other" is no small accomplishment. Marilyn vos Savant warns, "Emails, instant messaging, and cell phones give us fabulous communication ability, but because we live and work in our own little worlds, that communication is totally disorganized" (2013). It's no wonder George Bernard Shaw wryly observed, "The single biggest problem in communication is the illusion that it has taken place" (2013).

Conclusion

> Human beings are puzzling creatures. We are capable of the most magnificent personal and cultural accomplishments, yet we sometimes behave in ways that are not only irrational and short-sighted, but that also harm ourselves or others. We can experience uplifting emotions such as love, optimism, and awe, yet we also tie ourselves in knots of anxiety, anger, and despair. We sometimes stand up for our principles, but at other times, we behave contrary to our personal standards. We can remember thousands of trivial facts but forget an important appointment (Leary, 2012, 1).

17. Can We Know Ourselves?

self: a person as an individual; a person's special nature.
- Oxford American Dictionary

Inscribed in the forecourt of the Temple of Apollo at Delphi is *gnothi seauton* (know thyself). The same injunction serves as the motto of Hamilton College, a prestigious Upstate New York school. Saint Augustine prayed, "O God, I pray you let me know myself" (2009). From such convergent data, it seems that knowing one's self is important.

Polonius advised his son Laertes, "to thine own self be true," without telling him how to identify his true self. (Shakespeare, Act I, scene iii). Highly regarded among mental health professionals is a book written by psychiatrist James Masterson with the intriguing title, *The Search for the Real Self,* (1988). Another eminent psychiatrist, Thomas Szasz, has expressed his disagreement with Masterson: "But the self is not something one finds; it is something one creates" (1973, p. 49).

What makes you uniquely you and me uniquely me? By what means does each of us arrive at a sense of self? What does it mean when someone says, "I am not myself today," or "You don't seem like yourself"? Why is knowledge of the self important and what are the implications of not knowing one's self? These are the questions addressed in this chapter.

Is it our body that defines us?

If our body provides the truest measure of the self then continual redefinition is unavoidable. A spinal cord injury suffered in an equestrian accident in 1995 left actor Christopher Reeve a quadriplegic. The title of his memoir,

Still Me, testifies to his conviction that the accident that cost him his mobility did not take his identity from him. If a relatively minor bodily alteration like knee replacement does not redefine a person then, by logical extension, neither should a catastrophic condition like quadriplegia. This is not to say that adapting to an extreme bodily change is easily accomplished. A burn victim who suffers facial disfigurement or a soldier with multiple amputations experiences an assault upon the psyche as well as the body. As well, there are those who cannot weather the storm of such heartbreaking events and opt for suicide.

Is it our function that defines us?

On August 15, 1989 Dave Dravecky played his last baseball game. Pitching for the San Francisco Giants, he broke his left arm throwing the last pitch he would ever deliver. The cause of the fracture was a cancerous tumor that resisted radiation treatments and surgeries over the next two years. If Dravecky's identity resided in functioning as a major league baseball player, he lost himself on June 18, 1991 when his left arm and shoulder were amputated. But this is not what happened.

> Two months after the amputation, in August 1991, Dravecky and his wife, Jan, started Outreach of Hope, a Denver-based organization whose mission is to help people deal with the emotional and spiritual aspects of living with cancer, amputation, or serious illness. The foundation, which provides faith-based guidance and encouragement and sends baskets of print, audio, and video materials (including Dravecky's 1990 book, *Comeback*), has assisted more than 50,000 people over the last 18 years. ... (He says), "It's not what you

> do that matters most, but who you are. And who you are is about relationships" (Lemire, 2009, 108).

It is undeniable that accidents, diseases, and aging bring an end to certain activities, but they do not necessarily redefine the self. There is a difference between form and function. A hand does not cease to be a hand when it takes the form of a fist. If someone enters a house through a window, the window does not become a door. Metaphorically, it can be said of an over-the-hill athlete, "He's no longer himself." But metaphors are used to make comparisons, not factual statements. William James wrote metaphorically of self-identity in an 1878 letter to his wife:

> I have often thought that the best way to define a man's character would be to seek out the particular mental or moral attitude in which, when it came upon him, he felt himself most deeply and intensely active and alive. At such moments there is a voice inside which speaks and says: "This is the real me!" (Masterson, 1988, xii)

A moving exploration of function complicating self-definition is presented in the movie, "My Sister's Keeper." It is the story of the parents of a daughter with leukemia who produce a test-tube child intended as a perfect donor for their afflicted daughter, Kate. By age 11, the donor-child, Anna, has undergone several procedures for her ailing sister, including a bone marrow transplant. Eventually, when a kidney donation is imminent, Anna pursues medical emancipation from her parents to bring an end to the procedures. "My Sister's Keeper" raises the issue of function being so intermingled with identity that the two seem inseparable.

Is it our personality that defines us?

The definition of personality is, "an individual's characteristic pattern of thinking, feeling, and acting" (Myers, 2007, 595). When a man is referred to as "not being himself" it is most likely that he is deviating from his usual pattern of thinking, feeling, acting, or relating. In *Listening to Prozac*, psychiatrist Peter Kramer expressed his discomfort with personality altering medications:

> An indication of the power of medication to reshape a person's identity is contained in the sentence Tess (a patient) used when, eight months after first stopping Prozac, she telephoned to ask me whether she might resume the medication. She said, "I'm not myself."
>
> ... Tess had existed in one mental state for twenty or thirty years; then she felt briefly different on medication. Now that the old mental state was threatening to re-emerge - the one she had experienced nearly all her adult life - her response was "I am not myself." But who had she been all those years if not herself? Had the medication somehow removed a false self and replaced it with a true one? Might Tess, absent the intervention of the modern antidepressant, have lived her whole life a successful life, - perhaps, by external standards - and never been herself (18-19)?

Conceptually similar to Tess' situation is the phenomenon of some autistic children who discontinue being autistic when experiencing a high fever. (Unfortunately, this interruption is temporary.) What is common to both cases is a personality change. The characterization of people not being themselves is more likely associated with a deviation in personality rather than an alteration of body or function.

The story of Phineas Gage has been written large in both medical and psychiatric literature. In 1848 Gage, a

Vermont railroad worker, survived an explosion in which an iron rod passed through is head, entering at his left cheekbone and exiting out of the top of his skull. The path thus created enabled the physician who treated Gage to have his right and left forefingers meet inside of the injured man's head. The brain damage included a disconnection between the impulse firing limbic system and the restraining influence of the frontal cortex, radically reordering Gage's personality. Unable to control his behavior, Gage was rendered a creature of impulse, profoundly different from the calm, reliable gentleman he had been prior to the accident. In the wake of the accident, Phineas Gage was never again himself.

Consciousness is awareness. To be conscious is to be aware of one's self and surroundings. If all sensory modalities are intact, awareness is constituted, in part, by what is seen, heard, felt, smelled, and tasted. An abstruse component of consciousness is the inner life of imagination, ideas, and emotions. Sleep is an altered state of consciousness because of mental activity in the form of dreams. A person who has fainted or a boxer who has been knocked out are referred to as unconscious, but might actually be in an altered state of consciousness as well. Our awareness of ourselves – who we believe ourselves to be – drives our personality. In extraordinary circumstances self-consciousness is subject to variability and error.

The Three Christs of Ypsilanti is psychologist Milton Rokeach's case study of three residents of a Michigan psychiatric hospital who had the same delusion (1964). Each believed himself to be Jesus Christ. Curious about the effect the "three Christs" might have on each other, Dr. Rokeach arranged for the men to room together, work together, and have group therapy together. In spite of their frequent contact, each of the men maintained his claimed identity. If self-awareness is the actual measure of identity then each of these men is actually Jesus Christ. Yet, logically, at least two of them have to be wrong.

A rare and astonishing psychiatric phenomenon is a *psychogenic fugue*, a dissociative disorder in which an individual abandons one identity and assumes another, completely unaware of the previous one. Unlike the witness protection program, in which a new life is established intentionally with full consciousness of the previous one, the person experiencing psychogenic fugue strenuously maintains that the previous life never existed. Most of these cases last a few days, at most. (The writer Agatha Christie is believed to have had a psychogenic fugue for eleven days in 1926.) An exception is the case of Jody Roberts, a Tacoma, Washington journalist who disappeared in 1985. She was discovered in 1997, living a new life as Jane Dee Williams in Sitka, Alaska (Plummer, 1997).

More than body or function, it is personality that defines us. Phineas Gage and Christopher Reeve both experienced physical change, but only Reeve remained himself to himself and those who knew him. Neither Phineas Gage nor Dave Dravecky returned to his former work, but only Dravecky remained himself to himself and others. Following his accident, Gage took on an entirely different personality, as did the "three Christs" after they became delusional.

Why this Topic Merits Consideration

Self-esteem means self-estimation, and accurate assessment of the self is required for decision-making and overall life-management. "Man's got to know his limitations," Clint Eastwood admonished one of his movie adversaries (1973). In *Necessary Losses*, Judith Viorst encourages giving up on dreams that will never come true in order to invest in achievable goals. Distinguishing the attainable from the unattainable is sometimes not easily discerned, especially when people presumed to be knowledgeable are offering discouragement. Recall Dan Keplinger, featured in chapter fifteen ("Should we never give up on a dream?"). He is a real-life example of someone who followed Rudyard Kipling's poetic instruction to, "trust yourself when all men doubt you" (1910). Keplinger aspired to study art in college and pursue a career as a painter in spite of cerebral palsy. His continuous, full-body spasms require him to paint on his knees with his hands behind his back, using a paint brush protruding from a headband. To the amazement of his doubters, Keplinger, also known as "King Gimp," has succeeded. His paintings are bought by admirers of his work, many of whom are unaware of his cerebral palsy and the conditions under which he paints.

In addition to accurate self-esteem, an unwavering knowledge of what is valued is necessary for decision-making and life-management. A reciprocating action exists between desires and decision-making. Certainly, desires guide decision-making. But it is also true that decisions reinforce desires, thereby contributing to the formation of one's character. This is what the Trappist monk, Thomas Merton, had in mind when he wrote, "We are made in the image of what we desire" (2009).

Two literary examples of the interrelationship of desire, decision-making, and character are *The Bridges of Madison County's* Francesca Johnson and *Les Miserables'* Jean Valjean. Faced with abandoning her children and husband in order to run away with her lover, Kincaid, she chose to remain with her family. She declined the invitation to go with him with these words.

> Yes, it's boring in a way. My life, that is. It lacks romance, eroticism, dancing in the kitchen to candlelight, and the wonderful feel of a man who knows how to love a woman. Most of all, it lacks you. But

> there's this damn sense of responsibility I have. To Richard, to the children. Just my leaving, taking away my physical presence, would be enough for Richard. That alone might destroy him. ... As much as I want you and want to be with you and part of you, I can't tear myself away from the realness of my responsibilities. ... If I did leave now, those thoughts would turn me into something other than the woman you have come to love (Waller, 115 - 116).

Francesca intensely desired a life with Kincaid, but valued being an honorable, unselfish woman even more. Further, she recognized that if she chose to run away it would be the start of her becoming a different woman. She would be less the woman she could respect, as well as less the woman Kincaid had fallen in love with.

Les Miserables' protagonist, Jean Valjean, agonizes over whether or not to allow an innocent man to go to prison as a result of mistaken identity. Valjean, an escaped convict living under an alias, learns that a man has been taken erroneously as Jean Valjean and is soon to be re-sentenced and returned to prison. In the musical adaptation of Victor Hugo's classic, Valjean sings these words from "Who Am I?"

> Can I conceal myself for evermore? Pretend I'm not the man I was before? And must my name until I die be no more than an alibi? Must I lie? How can I ever face my fellow men? How can I ever face myself again? ... Who am I? I'm Jean Valjean! (Schonberg, 1988)

Like Francesca, Valjean chooses honorable confinement over dishonorable freedom, recognizing that to remain silent would irrevocably change him into the man he does not want to be.

Can we know ourselves?

Philosophical novelist Walker Percy posited that knowledge of the self is not easily attained: "Why is it that of all the billions and billions of strange objects in the cosmos – novas, pulsars, black holes – you are beyond doubt the strangest?" (1984). Nietzsche went even further, stating that self-knowledge is an impossibility: "We are unknown, we knowers, to ourselves ... each of us holds good to all eternity the motto: 'Each of us is farthest away from himself' - as far as ourselves are concerned we are not knowers" (2003, 1). The poet Robert Burns suggested that an understanding of how we appear to others would require divine empowerment: "O would some Power, the gift to give us, to see ourselves as others see us" (1786). While complete and impeccable self-knowledge is impossible, there are at least seven resources for acquiring some knowledge of the self.

Psychological Testing: The two categories of personality instruments used by mental health professionals are personality inventories and projective tests. Personality inventories present questions to the subjects. Two of the better known personality inventories are the MMPI (Minnesota Multiphasic Personality Inventory) and the Meyers-Briggs Type Inventory. Both have a long history of usage and enjoy high level of confidence among clinicians. Projective tests require subjects to respond to images with explanations or essays. Perhaps the best known of these tests is the Rorshach Inkblot Test in which subjects are asked, "What do you see?" when presented with a series of inkblots of various shapes. The TAT (Thematic Apperception Test) calls for subjects to write an essay based on a picture they have seen.

Convergent Data: Information provided by non-consulting parties is referred to as convergent data. According to psychologist Gordon Allport, there are 17,953 adjectives in the English language that describe human traits (1936). When two or more people who do not know each other make the same observation concerning an individual, the observation is likely accurate. For example, if a high school athletic coach, employer, and spouse all describe someone as having the trait of dependability it is likely an accurate observation.

Continuity of Behavior: A simple maxim is we are who we are most of the time. It is unfortunate for Bill Buckner that many baseball fans do not adhere to this aphorism. He had a major league career that spanned twenty-two seasons in which he amassed 2,715 hits, 1,208 runs batted in, 174 home runs, and a career batting average of .289. In 1980 he led the National League in batting with a .324 average. In spite of these impressive statistics, Buckner is best-known for an error he made in the 1986 World Series that cost the Boston Red Sox game six and, eventually, the world championship. Most of the time he was a very reliable first baseman, with a career fielding percentage of .992, which means that over twenty-two seasons he handled the baseball flawlessly over ninety-nine percent of the time. Notwithstanding, he is notorious for a ground ball that eluded his glove and went through his legs.

In contrast to Buckner is Dietrich Bonhoeffer, the Lutheran pastor who is remembered with great favor for his opposition to Adolf Hitler during the Nazi era. Bonhoeffer's participation in the failed assassination of Hitler led to the minister's arrest in 1943 and execution two years later. Among his influential writings is a poem, “Who Am I?” in which he wonders if he is the strong man who encourages his fellow prisoners or the frightened child who cries himself to sleep. He concludes that he is both and, at his best and worst, he is embraced by God. To study the life of Bonhoeffer is to become familiar with a man of conviction and courage. That is who he was most of the time, and those who think crying is a lapse in courage would do well to consider it is often the case that without fear courage is not possible.

Accomplishments: Colonel Jack Jacobs is a Medal of Honor recipient, recognized for heroism in Vietnam. When he is referred to as a Medal of Honor "winner" he makes the correction that the Medal of Honor is not something that is "won," it is earned. Achievements provide reliable indications of the true self. Neither Colonel Jacobs nor anyone familiar with his heroism can doubt that he has the qualities of courage, devotion to duty, and selflessness. There are some accomplishments that require certain characteristics. To lose one-hundred pounds requires commitment. To earn a place on the Dean's List also requires self-discipline as well as a measure of intelligence.

Anonymity: The difference between reputation and integrity is that the former refers to one's behavior when others are looking; the latter refers to one's behavior when no one else will know. A conversation on this point is found in *Plato's Republic* in which Socrates is challenged by Glaucon, who maintains that if a man could wear a ring that would make him invisible, that man would behave immorally. Socrates counters by arguing that even the impunity that would come with anonymity could not induce men of conscience to act immorally. How people behave when there is no foreseeable punishment or reward is another resource for self-knowledge. The Quaker philosopher David Elton Trueblood believed so strongly in the significance of acting without the possibility of reward that he wrote: "A man has made at least a start on discovering the meaning of human life when he plants shade trees under which he knows full well he will never sit" (1951).

Desire: People sacrifice for the things they value. As previously stated, "We are made in the image of what we desire" (Merton, 2009). Eric Liddell so valued his religious faith that he was prepared to sacrifice his opportunity for an Olympic gold medal by refusing to compete on the Sabbath. Such willingness defined Liddell as an authentic Christian.

Significant Decisions: Francesca Johnson and Jean Valjean have been offered as literary illustrations of decisions driven by personality as well as reinforcing it. Consider the following real life examples of people who demonstrated something about themselves with choices they made. Aron Ralston's self-amputation entitles him to never doubt that he is a true survivor with an astonishingly high pain tolerance (Malikow, 2008, 77-78). Clementina Geraci, a pregnant woman diagnosed with cancer, chose to not undergo the treatment that might have arrested the disease. In her last months of life, she knew with certainty of her maternal instinct and love for her son (Malikow, 2008, 12).

Conclusion

A metaphor is, "a figure of speech in which a term is transferred from the object it ordinarily designates to an object it may designate only by implicit comparison or analogy" (Morris, 1969, 825). Although the phrase, "I'm not myself" can refer to the body or functioning, it is more often the personality that is being referenced by this metaphor.

18. What Is the Place of Justice in the Human Predicament?

He has showed you, O man, what is good. And what does the Lord require of you? To act justly and to love mercy and to walk humbly with your God.

- Micah 6:8

Woe to you, scribes and Pharisees, hypocrites! For you tithe mint and dill and cummin, and have neglected the weightier provisions of the law: justice and mercy and faithfulness; but these are the things you should have done without neglecting the others. You blind guides, who strain out a gnat and swallow a camel.

- Jesus, Matthew 23:23,24

On June 2, 2010, Armando Gallaraga, a pitcher for the Detroit Tigers, retired twenty-six consecutive Cleveland Indians. He appeared to have achieved the so-called perfect game in which no batter reaches base when the twenty-seventh Indian batter hit a routine ground ball fielded by the Tigers' first baseman and tossed to Gallaraga covering first base for the final out. The celebration of this rare event turned to protest when first base umpire Jim Joyce made an obvious error and called the runner safe, depriving Gallaraga of what would have been the twenty-third perfect game in major league baseball's 135 year history.

Unlike football, baseball has no provision for a video tape review and reversal of an incorrect call by an umpire. When Joyce saw the replay after the game he admitted his error. The only person with the authority to overrule Joyce's call was the Commissioner of Major League Baseball, Bud

Selig. He refused to do so, reasoning it would be the first time a Commissioner overturned an umpire's judgment call and would establish an unwise precedent. Selig's decision was consistent with a principle of jurisprudence: *the law is concerned with neither right nor wrong – only precedent.* Was justice served by the Commissioner's decision? His critics argue that precedent should be set aside when it perpetuates an obvious injustice. Selig's supporters posit that without strict adherence to precedent there is no reliable system for dispensing justice.

Universal and Particular Justice

Aristotle's philosophy of justice, presented in the *Nichmachean Ethics*, makes a distinction between *universal justice* – that which is absolutely morally right, and *particular justice* – that which is right relative to a specific situation. In a perfect society moral absolutes could determine justice in every situation. However, specific situations sometimes require a deviation from moral absolutes if justice is to be served. For instance, truth-telling is a moral absolute and therefore a part of universal justice. Still, as much as honesty is respected as a virtue, there are times when withholding the truth or even lying might serve a greater good. If telling a lie would save a life it would be justifiable as a contribution to particular justice. Returning to the Commissioner's decision, his strict adherence to precedent is an instantiation of *universal justice*. Had he suspended the rule and overturned the umpire's call it wold have been an instantiation of *particular justice*.

Justice, one of the Four Cardinal Virtues, is sufficiently complicated to warrant three subcategories: *distributive, compensatory*, and *retributive*. The balance of this chapter addresses each of these separately.

Distributive Justice

Distributive justice is concerned with an equitable share of benefits and burdens. *Equal* and *equitable* are not synonyms. The former means "same in amount;" the latter means "proper and fair." Consider four people who receive the bill for the lunch they have enjoyed together. If they decide to pay *equally* they will simply add a tip to the amount and divide by four. If they determine the amount each will contribute according to the cost of each meal and drink, they will be contributing *equitably*.

A *Los Angeles Times* news story provides a remarkable example of a questionable distribution of burden.

> Father 30 Times Over Seeks Break in Child Support
>
> Desmond Hatchett, 33, is something of a local celebrity in Knoxville, Tenn. In 2009, in a t.v. interview, he proclaimed, "I'm done!" - that he wouldn't father more children. Now, with 30 children by 11 women, he wants a break on child-support payments. The youngest is a toddler; the oldest is 14.
>
> Hatchett has a minimum wage job, and he struggles to make ends meet. He's required to turn over 50 percent of his wages for chld support – the maximum under law (The Huffington Post, 05/18/12).

Hatchett, currently in prison and due for release in 2014, has been incarcerated previously for failure to pay child support. The burden of supporting the children he's fathered has fallen upon their mothers, charity, and public assistance.

A letter to the editor from a Syracuse, New York newspaper addresses the question: "Who decides what makes up a fair share?"

To the editor:

The next time I hear anyone say, The rich should pay their fair share," my hair is going to hurt. Surely, this is a vacuous statement. (Please refrain from saying, "Don't call me Shirley.") Who are "the rich" and how is this determined? What constitues a "fair share" and who decides?

The Marxist dictum, "From each according to his ability, to each according to his needs" disregards human nature by naively assuming people maximally produce while minimally benefitting. Ayn Rand produced two novels totaling 1,500 pages conveying the philosophy the rich have no philanthropic obligation to the poor. Similarly, Aesop implied that industrious ants are not morally required to subsidize indolent grasshoppers.

Like jurors betwixt dueling experts in a civil case, how are we to determine liability and what it should be? I suggest that before declaring how other people's wealth should be distributed, a bit of self-examination is in order. The Parable of the Good Samaritan (Luke 10:30-37) was told by Jesus in response to the question: "Who is my neighbor?" I submit here we have a starting point for answering the questions, "Who are the rich?" and, "What is their fair share?"

The next time you encounter a panhandler, consider how you are responding and, if you give, how much. Feeling rich? Giving a fair share? These questions are not intended to provoke guilt, but to clarify what you *really* believe. Then consider this thought from Herman Hesse: "The hardest road is the one that leads a man to himself" (*The Post Standard*, 11/18/11)

Concerning the fair distribution of benefit, there is no shortage of anecdotes describing the sense of entitlement felt by family members and friends of some lottery winners (Stossel, 1998). Requesters often express anger, indignation, or both if they are denied a gift or loan. Bob Harrell, a Texas Lotto winner committed suicide two years after winning $31 million (McVicker, 2000). William Post was on food stamps a year after winning $16.2 million in the Pennsylvania Lottery (Sullivan, 2006). Friends and family insisting on a share of the winnings contributed to the sad ending of both stories.

Compensatory Justice

Political philosopher John Rawls determined, "Procedural justice does not guarantee justice of outcome" (1971, II, 14). And ethics philosopher John Boatright has written:

> trial by jury ... is not a perfect procedure, but any alternative is worse. So unless we are willing to accept the verdicts of juries – even when the outcome is the conviction of an innocent person or the exoneration of a guilty one – the result is likely to be even more unjust outcomes (1993, 94).

Roy Brown is well aware of the criminal justice system's imperfection. In 2009 he received $2.6 million from the State of New York as compensation for fifteen years of wrongful imprisonment for a murder he did not commit. Was he fairly compensated?

Jonathan Harr's bestseller, *A Civil Action*, chronicles the lawsuit and settlement of a case of irresponsible waste disposal in Woburn, Massachusetts (1996). Eight cases of leukemia were connected to drinking water contaminated by chemical dumping. The $8 million settlement resulted in

$375,000 for each family. How much money is just compensation for a child victimized by cancer?

Is Alex Rodriguez's $250 million salary over ten years fair compensation for playing third base for the New York Yankees? Even "A Rod" might envy rapper and record producer Dr. Dre, who earned $110 million in 2012, the same year singer-songwriter Taylor Swift earned $57 million and country and western superstar Toby Keith took in $55 million (Greenburg, 2012). Compare these staggering amounts to the national average salary of a first-year teacher ($35,672) and consider if teachers are adequately compensated (National Education Association website, 2013).

Retributive Justice

"Let the punishment fit the crime" is a familiar aphorism to lawyers and laypersons alike. The Eighth Amendment to the *United States Constitution* prohibits "cruel and inhumane punishment" for violations of the law. *Retributive justice* is concerned with the question: What constitutes a fair punishment for a given crime?

The opening scene of the movie *The Godfather* is a distraught father meeting with Don Corleone, the Godfather. The man's daughter was savagely beaten by two men who attempted to rape her. She absorbed a horrific beating fending off the rape. The father's anguish was exacerbated when the two assailants received only a suspended sentence for their assault. He asks Don Corleone to have the young men killed. The Godfather refused, saying, "That's not justice; you're daughter is alive." He did agree, however, to arrange to have the young woman's beating replicated. The two young men received injury for injury the same beating they administered to man's daughter. This is talion law, characterized by the biblical instruction, "An eye for an eye ..." (Exodus 1:24).

An April, 2013 news story reported the sentencing of a man in Saudi Arabia to medical paralyzation. Ali Al-Khawahir, age 24, was found guilty of stabbing a man in the back, paralyzing him. The court ruled that Al-Khawahir must pay his victim approximately $250,000 or Al-Khawahir will have his spinal cord surgically cut to induce paralysis. Ann Harrison of Amnesty International expressed indignation at this instance of eye-for-eye justice: "That such a punishment might be implemented is utterly shocking, even in a context where flogging is frequently imposed as a punishment for some offenses, as happens in Saudi Arabia" (Grenoble, 2013).

Case Study: Is This Justice?

My whole life has been a waste – I've been a failure.

- Mike Tyson

The matter of Mr. Rose is now closed. It will be debated and discussed. Let no one think that it did not hurt baseball. That hurt will pass, however, as the great glory of the game asserts itself and a resilient institution goes forward. Let it also be clear that no individual is superior to the game.

- A. Bartlett Giamatti

Often, justice of any type (distributive, compensatory, or retributive) is not easily determined. Consider the following case of two great athletes, one of whom is in his sport's hall of fame and the other who is not.

On June 12, 2011 convicted rapist and former, self-proclaimed "Baddest Man on the Planet," Mike Tyson, was inducted into the International Boxing Hall of Fame. Twenty years earlier, on February 4, 1991, the governing body of the Baseball Hall of Fame determined that all names on major league baseball's *permanently ineligible list* were also permanently disqualified for consideration for enshrinement in

Cooperstown. Pete Rose, who had played more games (3,562) and had more hits (4,256) than any other player in major league history, was on that list. Barring a change of heart and vote by that governing board, Pete Rose will never be inducted into the Baseball Hall of Fame.

Before pursuing whether this state of affairs is equitable, a cursory review of some history is in order. In 1992 Mike Tyson was convicted of raping an 18 year-old beauty pageant contestant, Desiree Washington, in Indianapolis, Indiana. He subsequently served half of a six-year sentence before resuming his boxing career. This felony was hardly a blemish on an otherwise exemplary life. Other arrests and convictions preceded and followed the rape conviction. Further, even in the ring, Tyson could not evade ignominy. In his 1997 fight with Evander Holyfield, Tyson bit off one inch of Holyfield's ear in a third round clinch.

Two divorces would seem to disqualify Mike Tyson as a marriage counselor. His bankruptcy after having earned 300 million dollars over twenty years would seem to disqualify him as a financial advisor. However, being the youngest heavyweight champion in boxing history with an impressive record (50 wins in 58 fights, with 44 knockouts), entitles him to a place in boxing's Hall of Fame according to those entrusted with making such decisions.

In August of 1989 the Commissioner of Major League Baseball, A. Bartlett Giamatti, and Pete Rose reached an agreement on the matter of Rose's gambling on baseball games and his future participation in the sport. At that time an ongoing investigation al-ready had established that Rose had wagered on games in which he was involved when managing the Cincinnati Reds. (After denying he had bet on games, Rose eventually admitted to having done so, emphasizing that he never bet on the Reds to lose.) Giamatti agreed to discontinue the investigation if Rose would accept, without the option of appeal, his permanent ineligibility to participate in organized baseball.

Is it fair that Mike Tyson has the honor of hall of fame status and Pete Rose does not? This question cannot be addressed until two other questions are considered: What is justice? And, similarities notwithstanding, is likening Tyson and Rose an "apples and oranges" comparison?

What Is Justice?

Justice is the firm and continuous determination to render unto everyone that which is due. *Retributive justice* is concerned with determining penalties for transgressions. Often, it is no easy matter to determine the appropriate punishment for an offense. The decision-makers for the International Boxing Hall of Fame determined that excluding Mike Tyson owing to his criminal behavior outside of boxing would constitute an in-justice. Commissioner Giamatti and the governing body of the Baseball Hall of Fame decided otherwise for Pete Rose.

In the present case, has justice been served by one man receiving hall of fame recognition and the other being excluded? Is the only equitable determination of this honor the inductions of both or neither of these men? Has retributive justice been satisfied by Tyson's three-year incarceration for a criminal act and Rose's banishment for a rules violation? Is it defensible to claim that both men have been treated fairly?

Are These Two Cases Comparable?

It is tempting to compare the treatment these men have received from their respective sports. While it might be intuitive to claim that since Tyson has been inducted into his hall of fame, Rose should be inducted into his, such an assertion is simplistic. Their situations are similar, but not identical. There are differences that justify Tyson's inclusion and Rose's exclusion.

There is nothing in the mission statement of the International Boxing Hall of Fame that precludes Mike Tyson's election: "Our mission is to honor and preserve boxing's rich heritage, chronicle the achievements of those who excelled and provide an educational experience for our many visitors" (International Boxing Hall of Fame.com).

Returning to the question of equanimity, the differences between these two cases are sufficient to conclude that comparing Tyson's to Rose's is an "apples and oranges" exercise. Undisputedly, raping a woman is more reprehensible than betting on a baseball game. Nevertheless, Tyson's offenses have been criminal and addressed accordingly. His debts have been to society and he's paid them. In contrast, Rose's transgression concerns only baseball and his punishment was determined by major league baseball's system for dealing with such matters. Responsible for maintaining the integrity of the game in accordance with his judgment, Commissioner Gamatti investigated Rose's activity and reached an agreement with him. Those advocating for Rose's admission into the Hall of Fame seem to disregard that he refused the opportunity to formally refute the charges against him. (True, the Hall of Fame's decision came two years after his refusal. However, Rose had no reason to believe that he ever would be removed from baeball's ineligible list, given the precedent set by Commisionner Kensaw Mountain Landis when he banished "Shoeless" Joe Jackson in 1920.) In Commissioner Giamatti's statement to the press he described Rose's concession to permanent expulsion:

> The banishment for life of Pete Rose from baseball is the sad end of a sorry episode. One of the game's greatest players has engaged in a variety of acts which have stained the game, and he must now live with the

> consequences of those acts. By choosing not to come to a hearing before me, and by choosing not to offer any testimony or evidence contrary to the report of the special counsel to the commissioner, Mr. Rose has accepted baseball's ultimate sanction, lifetime ineligibility (1998, 117).

Pete Rose disregarded baseball's most unambiguous rule and gambled that either he would not be discovered or, if discovered, it would not matter. Some of his apologists have pathetically argued that it doesn't matter what Rose did to injure the game; his statistics justify his place in Cooperstown. However, Rose's induction would declare that individual accomplishments trump all other considerations – including indifference to the sport's integrity. Other apologists have argued that Rose's personal life is unrelated to his professional life and should have no bearing on his participation in baseball. This is a strange argument given that he wagered on baseball games while professionally engaged in the sport. (Noteworthy is that Mike Tyson never used either of these arguments to make a case for Hall of Fame selection. In fact, he never claimed he deserved this honor and seemed surprised when it came.)

Conclusion

Ultimately, the fairness of Tyson being "in" and Rose being "out" is a subjective judgment. For those who care enough about this issue to debate it, the position taken implies something about the one espousing it. (This is true for any moral stand taken.)

In closing, it's relevant to ask if more is expected of baseball players than boxers. "It ain't true, is it, Joe?" was not asked of Joe Louis, but Joe Jackson. The movie classic,

"Field of Dreams," based on W.P. Kinsella's novel, *Shoeless Joe*, includes Terance Mann's moving oration in which baseball, not boxing, " ... reminds us of all that was good and could be again" (1982). Of course, boxing has its devoted fans. But it does not have a place in the national heart in the way baseball does. Giamatti recognized this when he wrote:

> It's designed to break your heart. The game begins in the spring, when everything is new again, and it blossoms in the summer, filling afternoons and evenings, and as soon as the chill rains comes, it stops, and leaves you to face the fall alone (1998, 121).

19. What Do We Find Humorous and Why?

I remember the first time I ever made my mother laugh. It's lost on me what I said. I was very young. She laughed frequently, but I knew the difference between her social laugh and her really spontaneous laugh when she was caught off guard – which is the key to laughter, being caught off guard. I wouldn't have remembered it so well if it hadn't meant a lot to me.

- George Carlin

One can't express aggression and sexual drive directly, as it is prohibited in the society, so the desires get sublimated in telling "jokes." If you look at jokes, they are either about somebody getting hurt, or they have sexual connotation.

- Sigmund Freud

Who is the funniest person you know? Think of a joke or movie that made you laugh. What is the topic of that joke or movie and why did it make you laugh? Humor is something that induces laughter or amusement. It can be the product of design or a serendipitous event. The things that provoke laughter are numerous: cartoons, jokes, movies, parodies, puns, skits, songs, stand-up comedy, and even bumper stickers.

Humor is part of the human situation (universality) with cultural variation (particularity). Jokes that might be funny in one place or situation would not evoke laughter in another. "Blonde jokes" are virtually nonexistent in Sweden, where the population is largely blonde; lawyer jokes would not work in Italy, where attorneys are highly esteemed. A person suffering with Lou Gehrig's disease would not find a joke about amyotrophic lateral sclerosis funny. A mother who has lost a child in an automobile accident that involved a drunken driver would not be amused by a story that begins with the phrase, "Three guys go into a bar."

Since human beings could survive and reproduce without a sense of humor, laughter serves no evolutionary purpose. However, the same could be said about great books, paintings, and symphonies. Like works of art, humor enriches life. It also helps in managing stress and coping with tragedy. John F. Kennedy observed: "There are three things in life which are real: God, human folly, and laughter. Since the first two are beyond our comprehension, we must do what we can with the third" (2013). Humor was present even in the Holocaust. One survivor, Viktor Frankl, has written:

> Sometimes the other men invented amusing dreams, such as forecasting that during a future dinner engagement they might forget themselves when the soup was served and beg the hostess to ladle it "from the bottom."
>
> The attempts to develop a sense of humor and to see things in a humorous light is some kind of a trick learned while mastering the art of living. Yet it is possible to practice the art of living even in a concentration camp, although suffering is omnipresent (1946, 64).

Psychologist David Funder characterizes humor as an occurrence in which "a forbidden impulse comes out in a controlled manner" (2004, 335). Unlike a *parapraxis* (more commonly known as a "Freudian slip"), a joke is intentional and provides a release that mitigates anxiety. Freud believed this release accounts for the pleasure derived from humor. "We laugh at jokes if they express issues or conflicts that are unconsciously important but consciously unacceptable" (Cloninger, 2013, 26).

As stated above, Freud posited that jokes either have a sexual connotation or they concern somebody getting hurt. It would require a study of thousands of jokes cross-culturally in circulation to affirm or refute Freud's claim. However, judging from a smaller sample, his analysis does not seem to be a gross oversimplification. The theme of much humor is either sex or some form of illness or injury. In addition, there are at least six other recurring topics for humor: marriage, fear, miscommunication, stereotypes, exaggerations of everyday life, and parodies.

Recurring Topics

Sex is the topic of a well-known scene from the movie, "When Harry Met Sally." Over lunch in a crowded delicatessen, Billy Crystal (Harry) and Meg Ryan (Sally) have a disagreement when she claims that women often fake orgasms. He argues that an orgasm cannot be faked. To prove him wrong she convincingly feigns a spectacular orgasm, drawing the attention of everyone in the delicatessen. The comedian Woody Allen is well-known for lamenting his pathetic sex life with lines like, "The last time I was inside a woman was when I visited the Statue of Liberty" (2013).

Evidence of the popularity of illness and injury in humor is the frequency with which a joke begins with the phrase, "A man went to see his doctor." The comedy, "What About Bob?" features Bill Murray (Bob Wiley) as a psychiatric patient. It was favorably reviewed by movie critics and a box office success, grossing $93 million. Alcoholism, if considered a disease, is another type of illness frequently addressed in jokes.

Failing marriages, a source of considerable emotional pain in real life, also provide material for stand-up comedians.

"Take my wife … please!" is the signature line of Henny Youngman (2000). The late Rodney Dangerfield, who bemoaned, "I get no respect," included his wife among his detractors (2005). One of the most popular programs in radio history is "The Battling Bickersons," featuring John and Blanche engaging in one hilarious argument after another.

"Sinners in the Hands of an Angry God," a sermon preached in 1741 by the pastor and theologian Jonathan Edwards, remains a part of seminary education to the present day. In it Edwards painted a sobering, if not terrifying, picture of God's judgment and the reality of hell. Nevertheless, the fear of eternal damnation and deliverance to Satan have been the themes of many a joke, skit, and cartoon. Heaven, hell, God, and Satan were frequent subjects in Gary Larsen's internationally syndicated comic strip "The Far Side."

Humor often involves a verbal misunderstanding between two parties. Stated in a previous chapter is George Bernard Shaw's observation: "The single biggest problem in communication is the illusion that it has taken place" (2013). Miscommunication is the theme of the classic comedy routine, "Who's on First?" performed by Bud Abbott and Lou Costello. Don Novelli's hilarious collection of actual correspondence published as *The Lazlo Letters* includes an exchange between "Lazlo Toth" and the manufacturers of a bubble bath product:

> Dear Gentlemen:
>
> I want you to know first of all that I enjoy your product. It's always refreshing to spend some time in the tub with some bubbles.
>
> However, I must confess I am puzzled by some of the instructions on the box. It says; "KEEP DRY". How can you use it if you have to keep it dry?

> Thought you'd be interested to know someone like me caught the mistake. …
>
> Sincerely,
> Lazlo Toth (Novelli, 1977, 18)

The response from the Gold Seal Company's Consumer Relations Director implies that Lazlo Toth's letter was taken seriously:

> Dear Friend:
>
> Thank you for your recent letter regarding "MR. BUBBLE", which has been referred to this Consumer Relations Department for reply. …
>
> It is true, we do say on our box: Free Flowing "MR. BUBBLE" must be kept dry. By this statement we mean that the box of powder should be protected against dampness, such as moisture in the bathroom if the box is not put away. The box of "MR. BUBBLE" should be closed and placed in a cabinet until the next use. …
>
> Yours very truly,
> M. Hershey,
> Consumer Relations Dir.
> (Novelli, 1977, 19)

A similar "miscommunication" between consumer and product manufacturer is provided by the comedienne Sarah Silverman. She wondered why the aspirin bottle she purchased had the warning label: "KEEP AWAY FROM CHILDREN." Silverman was indignant: "I love children; I would never harm a child. Why do I have to stay away from them just because I'm taking an aspirin?" (2013)

Lawyers and blondes suffer jokes that reinforce unflattering stereotypes. Many stereotypical jokes are unquestionably offensive. Jokes that portray Jewish people as obsessed with money or people from West Virginia as uncultured and primitive are not innocuous.

George Carlin, Bill Cosby, Jerry Seinfeld, and Steve Wright are renown for exaggerating the mundane and reframing the ordinary in a way that evokes laughter. Consider these observations from Wright:

> I busted a mirror and got seven years bad luck.
> But my lawyer thinks he can get it down to five.
>
> I got a humidifier and dehumidifier for my birthday.
> I put them in the same room and let them fight it out.
>
> It's small world, but I'd hate to paint it.
>
> Everywhere is within walking distance if you've got enough time.
>
> What's another word for thesaurus? (2013)

A parody is a comic imitation of a well-known person, work of art, or situation. "Monty Python and the Search for the Holy Grail," "The Princess Bride," and "Blazing Saddles," are absurd representations, respectively, of heroic quests, romantic adventure, and the wild west. Scott Adams' comic strip, "Dilbert," is a parody of life in the corporate world.

The Dynamics of Humor

In addition to absurdity, surprise and cleverness evoke laughter. Hence the term "punch line" for a joke's climactic moment. The element of surprise is lost after hearing a joke for the first time. As George Carlin said, "the key to laughter (is) being caught off guard" (2008, 90). This is why it's not unusual for a joke to be introduced with the instruction, "Stop me if you've heard this one."

Similarly, the presentation of an unexpected idea or clever turn of a phrase can take the listener by surprise. Carlin was a master at this type of humor with questions like, "Why are we told to get on the plane? Isn't it safer to get in the plane?" and "Why does the weather report include the temperature at the airport? Who lives at the airport?" (2009).

Conclusion

As a species, we could survive and reproduce without humor, but we would not live as well. Likely this is what Francis Bacon had in mind when he wrote: "Imagination was given to man to compensate him for what he is not; a sense of humor to console him for what he is" (2013).

20. What Is the Place of Death in the Human Predicament?

Life is not lost by dying! Life is lost minute by minute, day by dragging day, in all the thousand, small, uncaring ways.

- Stephen Vincent Benet

I'm not afraid of death, I just don't want to be there when it happens to me.

- Woody Allen

Death is "the permanent cessation of all bodily processes" (*American Heritage Dictionary*, 1973, 339). It does not exist on a continuum. Just as it is impossible to be "a little bit pregnant," it is impossible to be "a little bit dead." "Temporarily dead" is as oxymoronic as "mostly dead." (This negates Miracle Max's diagnosis of Wesley in "The Princess Bride.") In this chapter death as a part of the human predicament is considered in terms of two questions: (1) Why is death often considered an unfortunate part of the human condition? (2) How might the inevitability of death be favorably viewed?

Death as an Unfortunate Inevitability

In his treatise on death, *Staring at the Sun: Overcoming the Terror of Death*, psychiatrist and philosopher Irvin Yalom posits:

> Self-awareness is a supreme gift, a treasure as precious as life. This is what makes us human. But it comes with a costly price: the wound of mortality.

> Our existence is forever shadowed by the knowledge that we will grow, blossom, and inevitability, diminish and die (2008, 1).

The philosopher Thomas Nagel wonders why the thought of death generates anxiety for so many people.

> ...if death is the unequivocal and permanent end of our existence, the question arises whether it is a bad thing to die. … most of us would not regard the temporary suspension of life, even for substantial intervals, as in itself a misfortune. If it ever happens that people could be frozen without reduction of conscious lifespan, it will be inappropriate to pity those who are temporarily out of circulation. … none of us existed before we were born (or conceived), but few regard that as a misfortune (1997, 25, 27).

Like Nagel, Sigmund Freud questioned why death should be a disturbing reality. In his essay, "On Transience," he admitted the sadness experienced at the death of a loved one or contemplation of our own end is an enigma:

> Mourning over the loss of something we have loved or admired seems so natural to the layman that he regards it as self-evident. But to psychologists, mourning is a great riddle, one of those phenomena which cannot themselves be explained but to which other obscurities can be traced back. We possess, as it seems, a certain amount of capacity for love - what we call libido - which in the earlier stages of development is directed toward our own ego. … But why it is that this detachment of libido from its objects should be a painful process is a mystery to us and we

> have not hitherto been able to frame any hypothesis to account for it (2008, 12).

Perhaps it is the uncertainty of that which follows life that makes death fore-boding. Few have expressed this fearful apprehension as eloquently as Shakespeare's Prince Hamlet:

> But that the dread of something after death,
> The undiscovered Country, from whose bourn
> No traveller returns, Puzzles the will
> And makes us bear those ills we have,
> Than fly to others that we know not of
> (Act III, scene 1).

In contrast to Hamlet, Epicurus expressed certainty that there is no existence after life and therefore nothing to fear: "Death does not concern us, because as long as we exist, death is not here. And when it does come, we no longer exist" (2013). The Stoic philosopher, Epictetus, placed death in the category of things that do not emanate from our own actions; even a person who commits suicide would have died eventually. Since death is outside of our control it should not be a source of rumination. He further believed that death itself is not terrifying; the terror comes from how we choose to think about it:

> Men are disturbed, not by things, but by the principles and notions which they form concerning things. Death, for instance, is not terrible, else it would have appeared so to Socrates. But the terror consists of our notions of death that is terrible (135 A.C.E., 5).

Philosopher and theologian David Elton Trueblood posited that death is tragic only when it concludes a life that has not been lived well. "It is surely not so bad to die, providing one has *really* lived before he dies. Life need not be long to be good, for indeed it cannot be long. The tragedy is not that all die, but that so many fail to really live" (1951, 164).

Death as a Favorable Inevitability

In his commencement address at Stanford University entrepreneur and inventor Steve Jobs designated death as "very likely the single best invention of life" (2005). He spoke favorably of death with this assessment:

> Remembering that I'll be dead soon is the single most important tool I've ever encountered to help me make the big choices in life. Because almost everything - all external expectations, all pride, all fear of embarrassment or failure - these things just fall away in the face of death, leaving only what is truly important.
>
> ... No one wants to die. Even people who want to go to heaven don't want to die to get there.
>
> ... Your time is limited, so don't waste it living someone else's life. Don't be trapped by dogma - which is living with the results of someone else's thinking. ... have the courage to follow your own heart and intuition. They somehow already know what you truly want to become. Everything else is secondary (2005).

Viktor Frankl also viewed death as potentially advantageous. He encouraged redeeming and optimizing life's three unavoidable tragedies – pain, guilt, and death:

> The third aspect of the tragic triad concerns death. But it concerns life as well, for at any time each of the moments of which life consists is dying, and that

> moment will never recur. And yet is not this transitoriness a reminder that challenges us to make the best possible use of each moment of our lives? It certainly is, and hence my imperative: *Live as if you were living for the second time and acted as wrongly the first time as you are about to act now* (1959, 175).

Yalom believes the awareness of death is one of four life issues that contributes to efficiency and effectiveness in psychotherapy. (The other three are free will and responsibility, the meaning of life, and self-disclosure.) He insists that death should be confronted like any other fear. Beyond that, it should be scrutinized and in so doing it "may serve as an awakening experience, a profoundly useful catalyst for major life changes (2008, 30).

For those who view life unfavorably, death provides welcome relief. In Cormac McCarthy's emotionally provocative play, *The Sunset Limited*, a nihilistic college professor, in a debate with a devout ex-convict, expresses his fervent desire to commit suicide:

> Show me a religion that prepares one for death. For nothingness. There's a church I might enter. Yours prepares one only for more life. If you could banish the fear of death from men's hearts they wouldn't live a day (2011).

With less intensity, but no less conviction, Shakespeare's Macbeth characterizes life as tedious and devoid of meaning:

> To-morrow, and to-morrow, and to-morrow,
> Creeps in this petty pace from day to day,
> To the last syllable of recorded time;
> And all our yesterdays have lighted fools

The way to dusty death. Out, out brief candle!
Life's but a walking shadow; a poor player.
That struts and frets his hour upon the stage,
And then is heard no more: it is a tale
Told by an idiot, full of sound and fury,
Signifying nothing.
(Act V, scene 5)

For some, like David Benatar, death is a desirable state although inferior to never existing at all. The introduction of his book, *Better Never to Have Been: The Harm of Coming into Existence*, includes this assertion:

> Each one of us was harmed by being brought into existence. That harm is not negligible, because the quality of even the best of lives is very bad – and considerably worse than most people recognize it to be. Although it is obviously too late to prevent our own existence, it is not too late to prevent the existence of future possible people. Creating new people is thus morally problematic (2006, vii).

Antinatalism, the philosophical position that places a negative value on birth, did not originate with Benatar. Twenty-five centuries earlier Sophocles opined, "Never to have been born is best. But if we see the light, the next best is quickly re-turning whence we came" (1996). The nineteenth century German poet, Heinrich Heine, expressed an antinatalistic thought in "Death and His Brother Sleep (Morphine)."

Sleep is good, death is better, but of course,
The best would be never to have been at all (2013).

Even noteworthy biblical figures expressed a preference for never having been. The "weeping prophet" Jeremiah lamented, "Cursed be the day on which I was born: let not the day on which my mother bore me be blessed" (Jeremiah 20:14). Another man of exemplary faith, Job, deplored his entrance into the world: "May the day of my birth perish and the night it was said, 'A boy is born!' That day, may it turn to darkness; may God not care about it; may no light shine upon it" (Job 3:3,4).

Conclusion

There are six possible responses to the question: *What is the afterlife state of human beings*? One is *agnosticism*, that is, to be without knowledge of "the undiscovered country, from whose bourn no traveller returns" (*Hamlet*, Act III, scene 1). A second is *annihilation* – to be reduced to nonexistence. Socrates spoke of this as one of two afterlife possibilities in the *Apology* when he said, "either the dead man wholly ceases to be and loses all consciousness, or, as we are told, it is a change and a migration of the soul to another place" (2012, 23). The story of the rich and the beggar, Lazarus, told by Jesus, provides a third afterlife possibility. At death, the rich man, who lived a life of self-absorbed indulgence, finds himself in hell; Lazarus is nestled in a place of comfort (Luke 16:19-31). This story conveys there is post-life judgment followed by reward or punishment. A fourth possibility is *universalism* – the belief that there is a heaven from which no one is excluded. This view maintains a benevolent God would not allow for a condition of eternal torment. *Transmigration of the soul,* often referred to as *reincarnation*, is a fifth belief and commonly associated with Hinduism and Buddhism.

A sixth afterlife belief is there is no afterlife because there is no death. The First Church of Christ Science (a.k.a.

Christian Science) teaches that death is an *illusion* – a misperception of reality. This abstruse doctrine requires an explanation. The Church's founder, Mary Baker Eddy, formalized the following ontological statement shortly after the Church's inception:

> Spirit is immortal truth; matter is mortal error. Spirit is the real and eternal; matter is the unreal and temporal. Spirit is God, and man is His image and likeness. Therefore, man is not material; he is spiritual (1994, 21).

Macbeth characterized life as a "walking shadow" (*Shakespeare*, Act V, scene 5). Eddy pronounced it a dream. She taught that just the experiences in a dream are not real, neither are the experiences of what seems to be material life. "Life in matter is a dream: sin, sickness, and death are this dream" (Eddy, 2009, 9). She believed a person who seems to die actually attains to another level of consciousness, a level that is inaccessible to those who have not so attained. Heaven is not a place; rather it is the blissful realization of oneness with God. Hell is not a location, but the anguished state of mind that believes sin, sickness, and death are real.

The German philosopher Martin Heidegger taught that death gives meaning to life. He believed without an awareness of death time would be nothing more than the movement of hands on a clock and turning over of a calendar's pages. Like Frankl and Jobs, Heidegger believed living under an unknowable, inescapable dead-line elevates time from worthless to valuable. Consciousness of death does more than enhance the value of time. It is a *sine qua non* for time to have any meaning or value at all.

Except for agnosticism, whatever a person believes about the afterlife is embraced by faith. Reportedly, Steve Jobs last words were, "Oh wow, oh wow, oh wow" (*Washing-*

ton Post, 10/31/2011). There isn't a single living human being who can state with certainty what Steve Jobs saw in his last moment of life. Until each of us arrives at that moment we would do well to live well. "The greatest dignity to be found in death is the dignity of the life that preceded it. This is a form of hope we can all achieve, and it is the most abiding of all. Hope resides in what our lives have been" (Nuland, 1993, 242)

Epilogue

What is the meaning of life?
(Why this unanswerable question has value.)

You will never live if you are looking for the meaning of life.
- Albert Camus

The purpose of life is to stay alive. Watch any animal in nature – all it tries to do is stay alive.
- Michael Crichton

What is the meaning of life? The writer Dale Long has addressed philosophy's fundamental question with these words:

> Why are we here? This is a timeless question that expresses humanity's fundamental desire to understand our collective existence and value.
>
> On a more personal level, why am I here? Many other people seem to have a pretty clear opinion of why I'm here. My wife believes I'm here to take out the garbage, help the children with their homework, and rub her feet. My boss believes I'm here to do my job and do it well. The person in the car behind me this morning looked as if she believed I was there to make her late (2012, p. 167).

Although clever, this assessment is hardly a definitive answer to the question of life's meaning. Long admitted this by adding, "However, while living up to everyone's expectations may give our existence purpose of a sort, it's not the same as figuring out our own answer about why we, personally, are here" (167).

The question, *What is the meaning of life?* brings to mind President Clinton's statement to a grand jury in the wake of his dalliance with Monica Lewinsky. It was there he said the oft quoted, "It depends on what the meaning of the word 'is' is." Similarly, the question of life's meaning depends on what the meaning of the word *meaning* is. In the present case, meaning is to be understood as, "what is intended to be; purpose; significance; end" (*American Heritage Dictionary*, 1969, 811). Hence, this question can be alternatively posed: *Is there an intention or purpose to the existence of human beings?*

Any claim to have an answer to this question arises from faith – a belief that does not rest on logical proof or material evidence. Apart from invoking faith, this question is unanswerable. Cheerfully, this does not render the question valueless. The purpose of this epilogue is to argue that the enduring existence of this unanswerable question implies the existence of God. As such, it constitutes a sixth argument in favor of the existence of a supernatural creator.

The five arguments traditionally presented to make the case for God's existence can be summarized as follows:

Cosmological: Anything that exists has a cause outside of itself. Nothing can be the cause of itself since nothing can exist and not exist simultaneously. Since the universe exists, it must have an agent that caused it. God is that causative agent. Ergo, God exists.

Teleological: The universe operates predictably rather than randomly. Predictability implies an intelligent designer. Ergo, God exists as the intelligent designer.

Ontological: God is the greatest conceivable being, possessing all good qualities to the ultimate degree. Existence is a good quality and greater than non-existence. Ergo, God exists.

Moral: Unless God exists, moral absolutes are an impossibility. (The only alternative would be moral relativism.) Moral absolutes do exist. Ergo, God exists.

Ethnological: All cultures across human history demonstrate a sense of the divine expressed in some form of religion. This convergent data is evidence that human beings have an innate sense of a supernatural being and spiritual realm. This implies a creator who intended this and designed human beings accordingly. Ergo, God exists.

To these five arguments (not proofs) a sixth can be added: The persistence of the unanswerable question of life's meaning provides an argument favoring the existence of God. Before proceeding to make this case, an overview of a secular understanding of life's meaning is in order.

A Secular Understanding of the Meaning of Life

Stated simply, all secular views of life's meaning have in common the belief that human beings are not created by a supernatural being for some divine purpose. For the secularist, there is no creator with a personality and plan. Rather, human beings are part of an evolutionary process that is indifferent to their existence. This impersonal process is the agency by which human beings have developed gradually to their present state.

Existentialism provides an understanding of life's meaning that is unmistakably secular. It is the philosophical movement associated with Martin Heidegger, Friedrich Nietzsche, Albert Camus, and Jean-Paul Sartre that emphasizes free will and personal responsibility. For the existentialist, there is no meaning to life apart from the meaning people bring to their lives. (Soren Kierkegaard, a Christian existentialist, is an exception to this description.) Further, the existentialist believes all of us can bring meaning to our lives regardless of our circumstances. Moreover, each of us is responsible for determining and living out the life that will be personally meaningful.

An existentialist, Viktor Frankl believed since life consists of thousands of situations, there is no single meaning to life but thousands of meanings. In his classic, *Man's Search for Meaning*, he wrote:

> I doubt whether a doctor can answer this question in general terms, For the meaning of life differs from man to man, from day to day and from hour to hour. What matters, therefore, is not the meaning of life in general but rather the specific meaning of a person's life at a given moment (1959, 130-131).

For this reason Frankl preferred the ten-thousand commandments to the Ten Commandments:

> In an age in which the Ten Commandments seem to many people to have lost their validity, man must learn to listen to the ten thousand commandments implied in the ten thousand situations of which his life consists (1969, x).

Professor Robert Solomon has characterized existentialism as "the philosophy of no excuses." The introduction to his course on existentialism includes this characterization:

> The message of existentialism ... is about as simple as can be. It is that every one of us, as an individual, is responsible – responsible for what we do, responsible for who we are, responsible for the way we face and deal with the world, responsible ultimately, for the way the world is. It is, in a very short phrase, the philosophy of "no excuses!" ... If there is a God, we choose to believe. If nature made us one way, it is up to us to decide what we are to do with what nature gives us – whether to go along or fight back, to modify or transcend nature (2000, 1).

Walt Whitman's poem, "O Me! O Life!" is a literary expression of existentialism. In the first seven lines the poet laments the apparent meaninglessness of life with phrases like, "the struggle ever renewed" and, "the empty and useless years." Then, dramatically, he implores readers to optimize their lives by recognizing their individuality and taking action:

> That you are here – that life exists and identity.
> That the powerful play goes on, and you will
> contribute a verse (1900, 166).

Existentialists are unimpressed by what people profess or predict for themselves. Sartre wrote, "Man is nothing else ... than the ensemble of his acts" (1957, 32). An individual's life is authenticated by what is done rather than what is said. A belief that is not expressed by action is inauthentic and not to be taken seriously. Thomas Szasz expressed agreement with Sartre with this observation: "People often say that this or that person has not yet found himself. But the self is not something one finds, it is something one creates" (1973, 49).

Natural selection is the principle that the behaviors and traits that will maximize a species' survival and reproduction will be passed on to succeeding generations. *Evolutionary psychology* is the study of the development of human behavior and the mind using the principle of natural selection. The question of life's meaning has no survival value and contributes nothing to reproduction. Hence, an evolutionist could not explain the existence and persistence of this question by saying it is integral to the perpetuation of the human species. In fact, to the contrary, it is counter-productive to the survival of many individuals whose existential angst culminates in their suicide. Further, an evolutionist might posit that this question once had survival value and, like appendices, wisdom teeth and other vestigial organs, no longer has a discernible function other than to keep philosophers occupied. If offered, this would be an argument from silence (*argumentum ex silentio*), by which a conclusion is derived from the absence of evidence rather than its presence.

A Sacred Understanding of the Meaning of Life

A sacred understanding of this question's durability is that human beings owe their existence to a creator who has an intention for their lives. The unanswerability of this question is intentional as well. The creator (God) has orchestrated the human condition in such a way that each of us must *discover* our own reason for being rather than *create* it as the existentialists maintain. Further, the process of discovering how our lives should be spent simultaneously contributes to each of us being the kind of person God intends. Lest this idea remain abstract, consider the Nobel laureate and humanitarian Albert Schweitzer. Reflecting on what he considered his privileged life, he determined to follow the principle of Jesus Christ:

"From everyone who has been given much, much will be demanded; and from the one who has been entrusted with much, much more will be asked" (Luke 12:48, *New International Version*). Schweitzer describes his day of decision in his memoir.

> One brilliant summer morning at Gunsbach, during the Whitsuntide holidays – it was in 1896 – as I awoke, the thought came to me that I must not accept this good fortune as a matter of course, but must give something in return.
>
> While outside the birds sang I reflected on this thought, and before I had gotten up I came to the conclusion that until I was thirty I could consider myself justified in devoting myself to scholarship and the arts, but after that I would devote myself directly to serving humanity. ...
>
> What the character of my future activities would be was not yet clear to me. ... Only one thing was certain, that it must be direct human service, however inconspicuous its sphere (1933, 82).

Schweitzer's service was as a medical missionary to the people of Lambarene in the rainforest of Central Africa. There he worked as a physician from 1913 until his death in 1965.

The existentialist believes an individual's essence or defining qualities are determined by action. Sartre communicated this in several of his works.

> What is meant here by saying existence precedes essence? It means that, first of all, man exists, turns up, appears on the scene, and, only afterwards defines himself (1957, 15).

The antithesis of existentialism is *essentialism*. The essentialist believes the purpose of an individual's life precedes that person's existence. The essentialist reverses the existentialist's mantra by asserting *essence precedes existence*. Albert Einstein expressed an essentialistic thought in an essay he wrote in 1931:

> Strange is our situation here upon the earth. Each of comes for a short visit, not knowing why, yet sometimes seeming to divine a purpose.
>
> From the standpoint of daily life, however, there is one thing we do know: that man is here for the sake of other men – above all for those upon whose smile and well-being our own happiness depends, and also for the countless unknown souls with whose fate we are connected by a bond of sympathy. Many times a day I realize how much of my own outer and inner life is built upon the labors of my fellow men, both living and dead, and how earnestly I must exert myself in order to give in return as much as I have received. My peace of mind is often troubled by the depressing sense that I have borrowed too heavily from the work of other men (1990, 3-4).

David Elton Trueblood also wrote of the meaning of life in juxtaposition to an obligation to others: "A man has at least made a start on discovering the meaning of human life when he plants shade trees under which he knows full well he will never sit" (1951, 58).

A knife provides an analogy that differentiates *essentialism* from *existentialism*. Consider two answers to this odd question: What makes a knife a knife? An essentialist would answer a knife is a knife owing to its construction. An implement for cutting is conceptualized by a knife-maker who then proceeds to fashion an instrument for cutting. An existentialist's answer would be, "It's merely an object until it cuts, it then becomes a knife." For the essentialist, a knife is a knife by design, even if it never cuts, cutting is its raison d'etre. For the existentialist, it is merely a nondescript object until it cuts; the act of cutting defines the object.

Knives, unlike human beings, have neither a mental life nor a free will. The sacred view of human beings is essentialistic, maintaining that each of us is responsible for *discovering* our purpose. The secular view is existential, positing that each of us is responsible for *creating* our purpose.

A theological statement articulating the sacred view of humanity is found in the New Testament. The Apostle Paul wrote to Christ-followers at Ephesus:

> For we are God's workmanship, created in Christ Jesus to do good works, which God prepared in advance for us to do (Ephesians 2:10, *New International Version*).

Another such statement is made in the Westminster Shorter Confession, a Protestant catechism:

> Question: What is the chief end of man?
> Answer: The chief end of man is to glorify God and enjoy him forever (1648, 1).

Granted, both of the above are no more specific than Einstein's vague notion of a purpose for his life or Trueblood's assertion concerning altruism. Nevertheless, all four communicate the idea of intentionality to our existence. It was this idea that prompted Schweitzer to discover his purpose and led to his calling to the people of Lambarene.

Conclusion

An excerpt from the novel, *Congo*, is quoted in the introduction to this essay: “The purpose of life is to stay alive” (Crichton, 2012). The fact that people kill themselves is ample evidence that this analysis is simplistic. Thirty-thousand suicides occur annually in the United States (Jamison, 1999, 24). If our lives could be reduced to a mere struggle for survival there would be no suicides.

Irvin Yalom posits there are four philosophical issues present in psychotherapy, one of which is *the meaning of life* (2000, 4-5). A psychiatrist of an earlier era, Carl Jung, also viewed life's meaning as integral to psychotherapy:

> Among my patients from many countries, all of them educated persons, there is a considerable number who came to see me, not because they were suffering from a neurosis, but because they could find no meaning in life ... When conscious life has lost its meaning and promise, it is as though a panic had broken loose and we heard the exclamation: “Let us eat and drink, for tomorrow we die!” It is in this mood, born of the meaninglessness of life, that causes the disturbance in the unconscious and provokes the painfully curbed impulses to break out anew (1933, 231,233).

Professor Jay L. Garfield of Smith College believes this question is sufficient to justify an entire course devoted to it:

> *What is the meaning of life*? It's a question every thoughtful person has pondered at one time or another. Indeed, it may be the biggest question of all. ... It is at once a profound and abstract question, and a deeply personal one. We want to understand the world in which we live, but we also want to understand how

> to make our lives as meaningful as possible; to not only know *why* we're living, but that we're doing it with intention, purpose, and ethical commitment (2012, 16).

This epilogue presents and supports the claim that the unanswerable question of life's meaning constitutes a sixth argument (not proof) for the existence of God. This question has persisted throughout the history of philosophy in various forms. It is implied by Aristotle's definition of happiness (*eudaimonia*) as well as his analysis that every event has four causes. The significance of this question resides not in its answer but in its endurance in spite of its unanswerability. Since it is not necessary for the survival of our species it is important for another reason. The contention of this epilogue is this question is innate rather than part of an evolutionary process. To appropriate a phrase from the Declaration of Independence, this question is "endowed by the Creator." This argument did not originate with this writer. It was stated sixteen centuries ago in far fewer words by Saint Augustine: "You have made us for yourself, O God, and our hearts are restless until they find their rest in you" (398 A.D.).

References

Preface

Brown, R. (1996). *Against my better judgment: An intimate memoir of an eminent gay psychologist*. New York: Harrington Park Press.

Dalai Lama (1999). *The art of happiness*. New York: Riverhead Books.

Windsinger, J. "Why I Write." Recovered from www.helium.com/users/24334 on May 30, 2012.

Introduction

Camus, A. (1953). *The myth of Sisyphus*. New York: Random House.

Hoffer, E. (1973). *Reflections on the human condition*. New York: harper & Row, Publishers.

Livgren, K. (1973). "Dust in the Wind." Label: Kirschner.

Solomon, R. (2000). *No excuses: Existentialism and the meaning of life*. Chantilly, VA: The Teaching Company.

1. What is a human being?

American Heritage Dictionary.(1973) Boston, MA: Houghton Mifflin Company.

Boswell, T. (2008). The life of Samuel Johnson. New York: Penguin Classics.

Burns, R. (1784). “Man Was Made to Mourn: A Dirge.”

Genesis 1:27. (1983). *New International Version*. Grand Rapids, MI: Zondervan Bible Publishers.

Isaiah 55:8,9. (1983). *New International Version*. Grand Rapids, MI: Zondervan Bible Publishers.

Katen, T.E. (1973). *Doing philosophy*. Englewood Cliffs, NJ: Prentice-Hall, Inc.

Myers, D. (2010). *Psychology (ninth edition)*. New York: Worth Publishers.

Pope, A. (1986). *Essay on man and other poems*. Mineola, NY: Dover Publications.

Plato (399 B.C.). *Apology*.

Schweitzer, A. (1933). *Out of my life and thought*. Baltimore, MD: John Hopkins University Press.

Torrey, E.F. (1986). *Witchdoctors and psychiatrists: The common roots of psychotherapy and its future*. Northvale, NJ: Jason Aronson, Inc.

Twentieth Century Fox (2004). “I, Robot.”

Wallace, D.F. (2006). "Consider the Lobster." *Consider the lobster and other essays.* New York: Little, Brown and Company.

Wells, D. Unpublished lecture given at Gordon-Conwell Theological Seminary (South Hamilton, MA) in a systematic theology class in the fall semester, 1982.

2. Is each of us unique?

American Heritage Dictionary. (1969). Boston, MA: Houghton Mifflin Company.

Camus, A.(1955). *The myth of Sisyphus.* New York: Random House.

Ephesians 2:10. *New International Version*. Grand Rapids, MI: Zondervan Bible Publishers.

Heideggar, M. (1927). *Being and time*. New York: Harper Perennials.

Leibniz, G. (1686). *Discourse on metaphysics*. Indianapolis, IN: Hackett Publishing Company.

Livinston, G. (2004). *Too soon old, too late smart*. New York: Marlowe & Company.

Myers, D. (2010). *Psychology (ninth edition)*. New York: Worth Publishers.

Reilly, R. "The Fight Before Christmas." *Sports Illustrated.* "The Life of Reilly." 12/27/99.

Shakespeare, W. (1623) *As you like it*. 2.7.139.

______________. (1611) Macbeth. 5.5.19-22.

Whitman, W. (2000). *The complete poems of Walt Whitman,* "O Me! O Life!" New York: Penguin Classics.

3. Do we have free will?

Ayer, A.J. (1969). "Freedom and Necessity." in *Philosophical essays*. New York. St. Martin's Press.

Cialdini, R. (1984). *Influence: The psychology of persuasion*. New York: Collins.

Darrow, C. "The State of Illinois vs. Nathan Leopold and Richard Loeb." August 22, 1924. Recovered from the Lerner and Loeb Homepage.

Fallon, J. and Aron, A. (2001). "Mysteries of Mating." The Learning Channel.Film Garden Entertainment, Inc.

Feinberg, J. and Shafer-Landeau, R. (2002). *Reason and Responsibility: Readings in some basic problems of philosophy*. Belmont, CA: Wadsworth/Thompson Learning.

Grim, P. (2008). *Philosophy of the mind: Brains, consciousness, and thinking Machines*. Chantilly, VA: The Teaching Company.

Holbach, P. (1770). *The illusion of free will. Reason and responsibility: Readings in some basic problems of philosophy*. 2002. Belmont, CA: Wadsworth/Thompson Learning.

Kant, I. (1998).. *Critique of pure reason*. Translated by Guyer, P. and Wood, A. Cambridge, UK: Cambridge University Press.

Katen, T. (1973). *Doing Philosophy*. Englewood Cliffs, NJ: Prentice-Hall.

Lewis, D.O. (1998). *Guilty by Reason of Insanity*. New York: The Ballantine Publishing Group.

Merton, R. The unanticipated consequences of purposeful social Interaction. *American Psychological Review*. Vol. 1, Issue 6, Dec. 1936.

Morris, T. (1999). *Philosophy for dummies*. Foster City, CA: IDG Books Worldwide.

Morris, W., Editor. (1969). *The American Heritage Dictionary of the English Language*. Boston, MA: Houghton Mifflin Company.

Pence, G. (2000). *A dictionary of common philosophical terms*. New York: McGraw-Hill.

Popkin, R. and Stroll, A. (1993). *Philosophy made simple.* New York: Bantam Doubleday Publishing.

Sacks, O. (1970). *The man who mistook his wife for his hat and other clinical tales*. New York: Summit Books.

Sherman v. United States. 356. U.S. 369. 1958

The Post Standard. Syracuse, NY. February 15, 2007.

4. How are we to understand human evil?

American Heritage Dictionary (1969). Boston, MA: Houghton-Mifflin Publishing.

Burke, E. (2012). Recovered from Brainy Quote website on January 20, 2012.

Dickens, C. (2011). *A Christmas Carol.* Charleston, SC: Createspace Publishing.

Hare, R. (1993). *Without conscience: The disturbing world of psychopaths among us*. New York: The Guilford Press.

May, R. (1982). The problem of evil: An open letter to Carl Rogers. *Journal of Humanistic Psychology*, 22, 10-21.

Milgram, S. (1974). *Obedience to authority*. New York: Harper & Row.

Morton, A. (2004). *On evil.* New York: Routledge.

Oliner, S. (2001, November). Ordinary Heroes. *Yes! Magazine.* Recovered from futurenet.org/can-love-save-the-world on December 15, 2009.

Peck, M.S. (1998). *The people of the lie: The hope for healing human evil.* New York: Touchstone.

Rogers, C.R. (1981, Summer). Notes on Rollo May. *Perspectives*, (2), 1. p. 16.

Rubenstein, R. (1987). *The cunning of history*. New York: Harper Perennial.

Schilling, S.P. (1977). *God and human anguish*. Nashville, TE: Abingdon Publishers.

Thayer, J. (1996). *Thayer's greek – english lexicon of the new testament*. Peabody, MA: Hendrickson Publishers.

Zimbardo, P. (1972, April.). Pathology of imprisonment. *Transaction/Society*. pp. 4-8.

5. Are there universal virtues?

Allport, G.W. & Odbert, H.S. (1936).Trait names: A psycho-lexical study. *Psychological Monographs: General And applied*, 47, 171-220. (1, Whole No. 211).

Hawthorne, N. (1978). *The scarlet letter*. New York: Norton.

Lickona, T. (2004). *Character matters: How to help our children develop good judgment, integrity, and other essential virtues*. New York: Simon and Schuster.

Martin, M. (1989). *Everyday morality: An introduction to applied ethics*. Belmont, CA: Wadsworth Publishing Company.

Matousek, M. (2011). *Ethical wisdom: What makes us good*. New York: Doubleday.

Seligman, M. (2002). Authentic happiness: Using the new positive psychology to realize your potential for lasting fulfillment. New York: Simon and Schuster.

6. Why are some people extraordinarily resilient and why do other people opt out of life?

Aristotle. (1999). *Nichomachean ethics*. Book VIII, 119. Indianapolis, IN: Hackett.

Armstrong, L. with Jenkins, S. (2000). *It's not about the bike: My journey back to life*. New York: Berkely Books.

Brown, H.J. (2012). www.motivatingquotes.com/ perseverance.htm. Recovered 06/18/2012.

Camus, A. (2011). Quote recovered from Motivational Memo website on January 1, 2011.

Charney, D. (2010). "This emotional life." PBS telecast, January 2010. Kunhardt McGee Production.

Cohen, R. (2004). *Blinsided: A reluctant memoir – living a life above illness*. New York: Harper Collins Publishers.

Coles, R. (1998). *The moral intelligence of children: How to raise a moral child.* New York: Random House.

Culver, J. (1989). "A deadly struggle against the sea." *People*. 08/21/1989.

Deford, F. (1981). "Kenny, dying young." *Sports Illustrated.* 03/09/1981.

Frankl, V. (1959). *Man's search for meaning*. New York: Washington Square Press.

Jamison, K. (1996). *Touched with fire: Manic depressive illness and the artistic temperment.* New York: Simon and Schuster: Free Press

Kelly, N. (2012). Unpublished interview conducted 06/16/2012.

King, S. (1982). *Rita Hayworth and shawshank redmption: Different seasons*. New York: Viking Press. Penguin Group.

Kipling, R. (1910). "If." *Rewards and Fairies*. Garden City, NY: Doubleday Page & Compnay.

Kushner, H. (2002). *Living a life that matters*. New York: Alfred A. Knopf. Random House.

Livingston, G. (2004). *Too soon old, too late smart*. New York: Marlow & Compnay.

Malikow, M. (2008). *Profiles in character: Twenty-six stories that will instruct and inspire teenagers*. Lanham, MD: University Press of America.

__________. (2009) *Suicidal thoughts: Essays on self-determined death*. Lanham, MD: Hamilton Books.

__________. (2010). *Being human: Philosophical reflections on psychological issues*. Lanham, MD: Hamilton Books.

Maltsberger, J. (1987). Keynote address at the annual meeting of the American Association of Suicidologists. Boston, MA.

Myers, D. (2007). *Psychology: Eighth Edition*. New York: Worth Publishers.

Shneidman, E. (2004). *Autopsy of a suicidal mind*. New York: Oxford University Press.

___________ . (1998). *The suicidal mind*. New York: Oxford University Press.

Shenk, J. (2005). "Lincoln's great depression." *The Atlantic Monthly*. October 2005.

Shumaker, B. (2010). "This emotional life." PBS telecast, January 2010. Kunhardt McGee Production.

Stingley, D. (1983). *Happy to be alive*. New York: Beaufort Books.

Swofford, A. (2012). "We pretend the vets don't even exist." *Newsweek*. 05/28/2012.

Wicker, C. (1989). "The man sentenced to life." Orlando Sentinel. 05/29/1989.

7. What is the place of emotions in the human predicament?

Aristotle. (1954). *Rhetoric. Book II. Topic 2*. Translated by Rhys Roberts. Los Angeles, CA: IndoEuropean Publishing Company.

Damasio, A. (1994). *Descartes error: Emotion, reason, and the human brain.* New York: Gossett/Trautman and Sons.

Dobos, R.J. (1950). *Louis Pasteur*. Boston: Little, Brown, and Company.

Funder, D. (2004). *The personality puzzle (third edition).* New York: W.W. Norton & Co.

Gray, T. (1742). "Ode on a distant prospect of Eaton College." Lines 99-100.

Hegel, G. (2012). www.cesareattolini.com/index.php/cn/companyprofileeng/the-origins-vincenzo. Recovered June 30, 2012.

"I, Robot." (2004). Twentieth Century Fox.

Katen, T.E. (1973). *Doing philosophy*. Englewood Cliffs, NJ: Prentice-Hall, Inc.

Myers, D. (2007). *Psychology (seventh edition).* New York: Worth Publishers.

Plutchik, R. (1980). *Emotion: Theory, research, and experience: Volume 1*. "Theories of emotion." New York: Academic.

Redfield-Jamison, K. (2004). *Exuberance: The passion for life*. New York: Vintage Books. Random House.

_________________. (1995). *An unquiet mind: A memoir of moods and madness*. New York: Vintage Books. Random House.

Sapolsky, R. (2004). *Why zebras don't get ulcers: The acclaimed guide to stress, stress related diseases, and coping*. New York: Henry Holt and Company.

Tennyson, A. (1850). "In memoriam: AHH."

"The Terminator." (1984). Orion Pictures.

van Gogh, V. (2012). Quoteland.com/author/Vincent-v-Gogh- Quotes/570. Recovered on 07/04/2012.

8. When is our behavior abnormal?

Ballard, C. (2008). Trevor Wikre sacrifices finger to keep playing football. *Sports illustrated.com*. 10/14/08.

Jacobells v. Ohio. 1964. 378 United States. 184.

Mack, J. (2009). An interview with John Mack. Recovered fromhttp://www.pbs.org./wgbh/nova/aliens/ johnmack.html. Recovered on 11/25/09.

Malikow, M. (2008). Cutting and running. *Profiles in character: Twenty-six stories that will instruct and inspire teenagers*. Lanham, MD: Roman and Little-field.

Rosenhan. (1973). "On being sane in an insane place." *Science*. 179 (4070). 250-258. 1/19/73.

Szasz, T. (1974). *The myth of mental illness: Foundations of a theory of personal conduct*. New York: Harper and Row.

Yalom, I. (2002). *The gift of therapy: An open letter to a new generation of therapists and their patients*. New York: Harper Collins Publishers.

9. What is heroism and why do we admire heroes?

Allport, G.W. & Odbert, H.S. (1936). "Trait names: A psycho-lexical study." *Psychological Monographs: General and Applied*, 47, 171 - 220. (1, Whole No. 211).

American Heritage Dictionary. (1973). New York: American Heritage Publishing Company.

Barkley, C. www.brainyquotes.com. Recovered 12/25/10.

Baum, L.F. (2000). *The wizard of Oz: 100th anniversary edition*. New York: HarperCollins.

Bunnell, D. (1974). "Tin Man." America (recording group).

Cabot, M. (2008). *The princess diaries*. New York: Harper Teen.

Hammond, A. & Bettis, J. (1988). "One Moment in Time." Houston, W. (recording artist).

Hartsock, D. "Couric & Company." CBSnews.com. May 10, 2010 (interview).

Homer, (1998). *The iliad*. Fagles, R. (translator).New York: Penguin Classics.

Hugo, V. (1987). *Les miserables*. New York: Penguin Books: Signet Classic.

Jamison, K. (1995). *An unquiet mind*. New York: Random House.

Lehrer, J. "Are heroes born or can they be made?" *The Wall Street Journal*. 12/11/10.

Malikow, M. (2010). *Being human: Philosophical reflections on psychological issues*. Lanham, MD: Rowman & Littlefield Publishing Group.

Martin, M. (1986). *Everyday morality: An introduction to applied ethics*. Belmont, CA: Wadsworth Publishing Company.

Ralston, A. (2004). *Between a rock and a hard place*. New York: Atria Books.

Shakespeare, W. *Hamlet*, 3.4.151.

Wheelock, C. (1910). *American education*. Volume XIV. Number 1. New York: New York Department of Education.

10. Are capable of meaningful change?

American Society for Aesthetic Plastic Surgery website. Statistic recovered on June 18, 2012.

"As Good as It Gets." (1997). New York: TriStar Pictures. Columbia Pictures.

Baldwin, J. (2012). Recovered from Brainy Quote website on June 18, 2012.

Baugh, L. with Eubanks, S. (1999). *Life out of the rough: An intimate portrait of Laura Baugh and her sobering journey*. Nashville, TE: Rutledge Hill Press.

Churchill, W. (1939). Quotation from an October, 1939 radio broadcast.

Frankl, V. (1984). *Man's search for meaning*. New York: Washington Square Press.

Freud, S. (1961). *Civilization and its discontents*. New York: W.W. Norton and Company.

Gardner, H. (2004). *Changing minds: The art and science of changing our own and other people's minds*. Boston, MA: Harvard Business School Press.

James, W. (1902). *The varieties of religious experience: A study in human nature*. New York: The Modern Library.

Lombardi, V. (2012). Recovered from Vince Lombardi Quotes website on June 18, 2012.

Malikow, M. (2012). *It's not too late: Making the most of the rest of your life*. Charleston, SC: Createspace Publishing.

Myers, D. (2011). *Psychology (tenth edition).* New York: Worth Publishers.

Niebuhr, R. (1943). The "Serenity Prayer" is commonly attributed to theologian Reinhold Niebuhr as part of a 1943 sermon.

Peck, M.S. Peck, S. (1995). *In search of stones*. New York: Hyperion Books.

________. (1984). *The road less travelled: The new psychology of love, traditional values, and spiritual growth*. New York: Simon and Schuster.

Rosenbaum, E. (1988). *A taste of my own medicine: When a doctor is the patient*. New York: Random House.

Santana, C. (1970). "Evil ways." Written by Henry, C. Recorded by Columbia Records.

Seligman, M. (1993). *What you can change ... and what you can't: The complete guide to self-improvement.* New York: Vintage Books. Random House.

Spence, G. (1996). *The making of a country lawyer: An autobiography*. New York: St. Martin's Press.

Szasz, T. (1973). *The second sin*. Garden City, NY: Anchor Press. Doubleday and Company, Inc.

Wholey, D. (1998). *The miracle of change: The path to self development and spiritual growth*. New York: Simon and Schuster.

11. What is the place of sex in the human situation?

"A League of Their Own." (1992). Columbia Pictures.

Freud, S.. "A letter from Freud."*American Journal of Psychiatry*. 107, 786=787. 04/09/1935.

Sarason, I. And Sarason, B. (1996). *Abnormal psychology: The problem of maladaptive behavior*. Upper Saddle River, NJ: Prentice – Hall, Inc.

Seligman, M. (1993). *What you can change and what you can't. The complete guide to self-improvement*. New York: Random House.

"Sex unknown." (2001). NOVA.

"The difference between men and women." (2006). Princeton, NJ: Films for the Humanities and Sciences. Produced by ABC News.

12. What is the place of love in the human predicament?

Carroll, A., Editor (1997). Letters of a nation. New York: Broadway Books.

Greeley, A. (1983). *A piece of my mind ... on just about everything*. Garden City, NY: Doubleday and Company, Inc.

"Hud." (1963). Paramount Pictures.

Karr, M. (2009). "Reference to ex-man's next." *Sinners welcome*. New York: HarperCollins.

King, M.L. (1963). “I have a dream.” Speech delivered August 28, 1963 in Washington, DC on the occasion of the Civil Rights March.

McMurtry, L. (1961). *Hud.* United Kingdom: Sphere Books.

Morris, W., editor.(1969).*The American heritage dictionary of the English language*. Boston, MA: Houghton Mifflin Company.

Myers, D. (2012). *Psychology. Tenth edition*. New York: Worth Publishers.

Russell, B. (1975). *Autobiography*. New York: Routledge Classics.

Silverstein, S. (1964). *The giving tree*. New York: Harper & Row, Publishers.

Viorst, J. (1986). *Necessary losses: The loves, illusions, dependencies and impossible expectations that all of us have to give up in order to grow*. New York: Simon and Schuster.

13. What does it mean to be religious?

Alexander, E. (2012). *Proof of heaven: A neurosurgeon's journey into the afterlife*. New York: Simon and Schuster.

Berger, P. (1969). *A rumor of angels: Modern society and the rediscovery of the supernatural*. New York: Doubleday and Company, Inc.

Calaprice, A. Editor. (2002). *Dear Professor Einstein: Albert Einstein's letters to and from children*. Amherst, NY:Promethius Books.

Eliade, M. (1987). *The sacred and profane: The nature of religion*. New York: Harcourt, Brace, and Jovanonich.

Freud, S. (1961). *The future of an illusion*. New York: W.W. Norton and Company.

_______. (1927). *The future of an illusion*. London, UK: Hogarth Press.

Peck, S. (1993). *Further along the road less traveled: The unending journey toward spiritual growth*. New York: Touchstone Books.

Ponomareff and Bryson (2006).*The curve of the sacred: An exploration of human spirituality*. Value Inquiry Book Series. Volume 178.

Rogers, W. (2012). Recovered from Brainy Quote website on June 19, 2012.

Stevens, A. (1994). *Jung: A very short introduction*. New York: Oxford University Press.

14. How does pleasure work?

Allport, G. & Odbert, H.S. (1936). "Trait names: A psycholexical study." *Psychological monographs: General and applied*, 47. 171-220, (1 Whole No. 211).

Blackburn, S. (2009). *The big questions*. London, UK: Quercus Publishing.

Bloom, P. (2010). *How pleasure works: The new science of why we like what we like*. New York: W.W. Norton and Company.

Descartes, R. (1999). Clarke, D., Translator. *Meditations: And other metaphysical writings*. New York: Penguin Classics.

Hume, D. (1967). *A treatise of human nature*. Oxford, UK: Oxford University Press.

_______. (1985). "Of the standard of taste." from *Essays, moral, political, and literary*. Miller, E., Editor. Indianapolis, IN: IndianapolisLiberty Fund.

Kant, I. (1952). *The critique of pure judgment*. Merideth, J., translator. Oxford, UK: Oxford University Press.

Lafave, K.O. (2010). "Life as human." TED. 03/13/2010.

Malikow, M. (2009). *Philosophy 101: A primer for the apathetic or struggling student*. Lanham, MD: University Press of America.

Mullins, A. (2009). "How my legs give me super powers." TED Conference. February 2009. Recovered from Quotations Page website on May 31, 2011.

Ross, J. (2013). "The senses and the psychology of quality." Recovered from the Enology International website on June 21, 2013.

Shakespeare, W. (1597). *Romeo and Juliet.* Act II. Scene 2.

_____________. (circa 1596). *The merchant of Venice.* Act I, scene 1.

"The Prince of Tides." (1991). Based on the novel, *The Prince of Tides*. Pat Conroy, author. Columbia Pictures.

Wicker, C. (1989). "The man sentenced to life." Orlando Sentinel. 05/29/1989.

15. Should we never give up on a dream?

Browning, R. (1855). "Andrea Del Sarto." (aka ""The Faultless Painter"). Recovered from the University of Toronto on-line Representative Poetry on June 25, 2013.

Burroughs, A. (2012). *This is how: Help for the self in overcoming*. New York: St. Martin's Press.

Hartman, D. (1976). "Everyone is handicapped in some way." *People Magazine.* Volume 6, Number 15.October 11, 1976.

Henley, W. (2003). "Invictus." Recovered from Poem Hunter.com website posting of January 3, 2003 on June 25, 2013.

Kipling, R. (2002). "If." Recovered from Poem Hunter.com website posting of December 31, 2002 on June 25, 2013.

Leibs, A. (2009). "Cerebral palsy no barrier to art: Dan Kepplinger's paintings explore the experience of disability. Vancouver, BK: Suite 101.com. Com Media, Inc. August 4, 2009.

"Rocky." (1976). United Artists: Chartoff-Winkler Productions.

"The Cinderella Man." (2005). Miramax Films.

Viorst, J. (1986). *Necessary losses: The loves, illusions, dependencies, and impossible expectations that all of us have to give up in order to grow*. New York: Simon and Schuster.

Whittier, J. (2013). "Mayde Miller." Recovered from ThinkExist.com website on June 25, 2012.

16. What does it mean to be a *homo sapien*?

Collins, B. (2001). *Sailing alone around the room: New and selected poems*. New York: Randon House.

Cronkite, K. (1994). *On the edge of darkness: Conversations about conquering depression*. New York: Doubleday Dell Publishing Group.

Horowitz, J. (2003). "Ten foods that pack a wallop." *Time*. 159(3). January 21, 2006.

Hunter, I. (1998). *The very best of Malcolm Muggeridge*. Vancouver, BC: Regent College Publishing.

R.D. Laing. (1969). *Self and others*. New York: Pelican Books.

Leary, M., Editor. (2001). *Interpersonal rejection*. New York: Oxford University Press.

Malikow, M. (2006). *Teachers for life: Advice and methods gathered along the way*. Lanham, MD: Rowman and Littlefield Education Publishing.

Murray, H. (1938). *Explorations in personality*. New York: Oxford University Press.

Peck, S. (1995). *In search of stones*. New York: Hyperion Books.

Plato (399 B.C.) *The apology*. Charleston, SC: Createspace Independent Publishing Platform. 2013.

Rand, A. (2013). Recovered from Brainy Quote website on June 17, 2013.

Shaw, G. (2013). Recovered from Brainy Quote website on 06/08/2013.

Twain, M. (1970). *Man is the only animal that blushes ... or needs to: The wisdom of Mark Twain*. Stanyan Books.

Vos Savante, M. (2013). Recovered from Brainy Quote website on February 19, 2013.

Wallace, D. (2009). *This is water: Some thoughts delivered on a significant occasion, about living a compassionate life*. New York: Little, Brown, and Company.

17. Can we know ourselves?

Allport, G.W. & Odbert, H.S. (1936). Trait-names: A psycho-lexical study. *Psychological Monographs: General and Applied*, 47, 171-220. (1, Whole No. 211).

Augustine. Recovered from Rev. Fr. Benedict Hughes, CMRI. Sermon: "Lord That I May Know Myself ..." CMRI Index. August 3, 2009.

Burns, R. (1786) "To a louse." verse 8.

Cohen, R. (2004). *Blindsided: A reluctant memoir*. New York: Harper Collins Publishers.

Eastwood, C. "Magnum Force." (1973). Warner Brothers.

Kipling, R. (1910). "If." Garden City, NY: Doubleday.

Kramer, P. (1997). *Listening to prozac*. New York: Penguin Books.

Lemire, J. Lost and found. Sports Illustrated. July 13, 2009.

Malikow, M. (2008). *Profiles in character: Twenty-six stories that will instruct and inspire teenagers*. Lanham, MD: University Press of America.

Masterson, J. (1988). *The search for the real self: Unmasking the personality disorders of our age*. New York: The Free Press.

Merton,T. Recovered from: http://moonriver.spaces.live.com. August 3, 2009.

Morris, W. (Editor). (1969). *The American heritage dictionary of the English language*. Boston, MA: Houghton - Mifflin.

Myers, D. (2007). *Psychology*. New York: Worth Publishers.

Nietzsche, F. (2003). *On a geneaology of morals: A polemic.* Translated by Douglas Smith. London, UK: Oxford University Classics.

Percy, W. (1984). *Lost in the cosmos: The last self help book.* New York: Simon and Schuster.

Plummer, W. People Magazine. August 18, 1997. Volume 48, Number 7.

Rokeach, M. (1964). *The three Christs of Ypsilanti*. New York: Columbia University Press.

Schonberg, C.M. (1988). "Who Am I?" *Les Miserables*.

Shakespeare, W. *Hamlet*. Act I. scene iii.

Szasz, T. (1973). *The second sin*. Garden City, NY: Anchor Press.

Trueblood, D.E. (1951). *The life we prize*. New York: Harper & Brothers.

Waller, R.J. (1992). *The bridges of madison county*. New York. Warner Books, Inc.

18. What is the place of justice in the human situation?

Boatright, J. (1993). *Ethics and the conduct of business.* New York: Prentice-Hall, Inc.

Giamatti, A. (1998). *A great and glorious game*. Chapel Hill, NC: Algonquin Books.

Grenoble, R. (2013). "Ali Al-Khawajir, Saudi man sentenced to be paralyzed in 'eye for eye justice." *The Huffington Post*. April 4, 2013.

Harr, J. (1996). *A civil action*. New York: Vintage Press. Random House.

International Boxing Hall of Fame website. IBOF.com. Recovered June 15, 2013.

Kinsella (1982). *Shoeless Joe*. New York: Houghton Mifflin.

McVicker. (2000)."Billie Bob's misfortune." *The Houston Press*. February 10, 2000.

National Education Association website. Recovered on June 15, 2013.

Rawls, J. (1971). *A theory of justice*. Cambridge, MA: Harvard University Press.

Stossel, J. (1998). "The mystery of happiness: Who has it and how to get it." ABC News Special. Airing date: January 22, 1998.

Sullivan, P. "William 'Bud' Post III: Unhappy lottery winner. The Washington Post. January 20, 2013.

The Huffington Post (2012). "Father thirty times over seeks break in child support." Reported in The Los Angeles Times on May 18, 2012.

The Post Standard (2012). "Who decides what makes up a fair share?" Malikow, M. November 18, 2011.

19. What do we find humorous and why?

Allen, W. (2013). Recovered from Brainy Quote websiteon 06/08/2013.

Bacon, F. (2013). Recovered from Brainy Quote website on 06/08/2013.

Carlin, G. (2008). *Psychology today*. September/October 2008.

________. (2009). "FM & AM." audio cd. laugh.com.

Cloninger, S. (2013). *Theories of personality: Understanding persons (sixth edition).* Upper Saddle River, NJ: Pearson Higher Education Press.

Dangerfield, R. (2005). *It ain't easy being me: A lifetime of no respect but plenty of sex and drugs*. New York: HarperCollins.

Frankl, V. (1946). *Man's search for meaning*. New York: Washington Square Press.

Funder, D. (2004). *The personality puzzle (third edition).* New York: W.W. Norton and Company.

Kennedy, J.F. (2013). JFK quote page. Recovered 04/19/2013 from scmidnightflyer.com/jfk.html.

Novelli, D. (1977).*The Lazlo letters*. New York: Workman Publishing Company.

Shaw, G. (2013). Recovered from Brainy Quote website on 06/08/2013.

Silverman, S. (2013). Recovered from an unrecorded televised stand up comedy routine.

Wright, S. (2013). Recovered from Brainy Quote website on 06/08/2013.

Youngman, H. (2000). *Take my wife, please: Henry Youngman's giant book of jokes*. New York: Citadel Press. Kensington Publishing Company.

20. What is the place of death in the human predicament?

American Heritage Dictionary. (1973). Boston: Houghton Mifflin Company.

Benatar, D. (2006). *Better never to have been: The harm of coming into existence*. Oxford, UK: Oxford University Press.

Eddy, M. (1994). *Science and health with key to the scriptures*. Boston: Christian Science Board of Directors.

_______. (2009). *Christian health*. Boston: Christian Science Publishing Society.

Epictetus. (2013). Recovered from brainy-quote.com/quotes/authors/e/epictetus on 05/15/2013.

Epicurus. (2013). Recovered from brainy-quote.com/quotes/authors/e/epicurus on 05/15/2013.

Frankl, V. (1959). *Man's search for meaning*. New York: Washington Square Press.

Freud, S. (2008). *On transience*. Translated by J. Strachey. New York: Riverhead Books.

Heine, H. "Death and his brother sleep." lines 15-16. *Morphine*. Recovered from PoemHunter.com on 05/15/2013.

Jobs, S. (2005). *Stanford News*. 06/12/2005.

______. *The Washington Post*. 10/31/2011.

McCarthy, C. (2011). *The sunset limited*. HBO Movies.

Nagel, T. (1997). "Death." *The grim reader*. Spiegel, M and Tristman, R., editors. New York: Anchor Books.

Nuland, S. (1993). *How we die: Reflections on death's final chapter*. New York: Random House.

Shakespeare, W. (2013). *The complete works of William Shakespeare*, seventh edition. Bevington, D., Editor. London, UK: Longman Publishing.

Socrates. *Fifty readings in philosophy*, fourth edition. Abel, D., editor. New York: McGraw – Hill.

Sophocles. *Oedipus at colonus*. Lines 1224-31. Greene, D., editor and translator. Chicago, IL: University of Chicago Press.

Trueblood, D. (1951). *The life we prize*. New York: Harper and Brothers Publishers.

Yalom, I. *Staring at the sun: Overcoming the terror of death*. San Francisco, CA: Jossey-Bass. Wiley Publishing.

Epilogue: What is the meaning of life? (Why this unanswerable question has value.)

American Heritage Dictionary. (1969). William Morris, Editor. New York. American Heritage Publishing Company.

Augustine(circa 398 A.D.) Reprinted in 1960 by New York: Image Books.

Crichton, M. quotation recovered from Goodreads website on May 21, 2012.

Einstein, A. (1931). "From living philosophies." *Living philosophies: The reflections of some eminent men and women of our time*. New York: Doubleday.

Frankl, V. (1959) *Man's search for meaning*. New York. Washington Square Press.

_________ (1969) *The will to meaning: Foundations and applications of logotherapy.* New York: Penguin Books.

Garfield, J. (2012). *The meaning of life: Perspectives from the world's intellectual traditions*. Chantilly, VA: The Teaching Company.

Jamison, K. (1999). *Night falls fast: Understanding suicide.* New York: Alfred A. Knopf.

Jung, C. (1933). *Modern man in search of a soul.* New York: Harvest Books.

Long, D. (2011). "Why are we here?" from *This I believe: Life lessons*. Dan Gediman, John Gregory, and Mary Jo Gediman, Edtors. Hoboken, NJ: John Wiley and Sons.

Sartre, J. (1957). *Existentialism and human emotions*. New York: Kensington Publishing Corporation.

Schweitzer, A. (1931). *Out of my life and thought*. Translated by Antje Bultman Lemke. Baltimore, MD: Johns Hopkins University Press.

Solomon, R. (2000). *No excuses: Existentialism and the meaning of life.* Chantilly, VA: The Teaching Company.

Szasz, T. (1973). *The second sin*. Garden City, NY: The Anchor Press.

Trueblood, D. (1951). *The life we prize*. New York: Harper & Brothers Publishers.

Whitman, W. (1900). *Leaves of grass*. Acquired May 17. 2012 from Great Books Online.

Yalom, I. (2000). *Love's executioner and other tales of psychotherapy*. New York: Harper Perennial.

About the Author

Max Malikow is on the faculty of the Renee Crown Honors Program of Syracuse University and an Adjunct Assistant Professor of Philosophy at LeMoyne College. He earned his M.A. from Gordon-Conwell Theological Seminary and Th.D. from Boston University.

His other books include *Being Human: Philosophical Reflections on Psychological Issues*, *Philosophy 101: A Primer for the Apathetic or Struggling Student*, *Philosophy Reader: Essays and Articles for Thought and Discussion*, *Profiles in Character*, and *Suicidal Thoughts: Essays on Self-Determined Death*. He is a practicing psychotherapist in Syracuse, New York.

CPSIA information can be obtained at www.ICGtesting.com
Printed in the USA
LVOW01s0852060915

453023LV00020B/626/P